THE LITTLE BOOK OF
JEWISH
CELEBRATIONS

RONALD TAUBER

ILLUSTRATED BY YELENA BRYKSENKOVA

CHRONICLE BOOKS

SAN FRANCISCO

Library of Congress Cataloging-in-Publication Data:
Tauber, Ronald.
 The Little book of Jewish celebrations / Ronald Tauber.
     pages cm
 ISBN 978-1-4521-3141-2
 1. Fasts and feasts—Judaism. I. Title.

 BM690.T455 2014
 296.4'3—dc23

                        2013040513

Manufactured in China

Designed by Allison Weiner
Text by Ronald Tauber

10 9 8 7 6 5 4 3 2

Chronicle Books LLC
680 Second Street
San Francisco, California 94107
www.chroniclebooks.com

This book is dedicated to my wife, children, and grandchildren, who make all of our celebrations joyful.

CONTENTS

INTRODUCTION

And you shall be altogether joyful.

—DEUTERONOMY 16:15

Jewish holidays and days of celebration are warm, joyous affairs centered around the foundations of Jewish life: family, prayer, and festive meals. From the Passover seder table to the breaking of a glass under the chuppah at a wedding, most of the celebrations commemorate events in Jewish history recounted in the Bible and include traditions that have been practiced over more than two millennia. The Sabbath, major holy days, and rites of passage provide the fuel that have kept the Jewish faith glowing, even in times of strife. This book is a tribute to the time-honored customs that enrich Jewish life, connecting Jews from all corners of the world in celebration. In it you'll find the customs and traditions associated with each special day, its scriptural sources and origins, and the important words related to the holiday. Refer to these pages to revel in the meaning of each holiday, or to learn of the customs associated with a lifecycle event.

HOLIDAYS

While each holiday has its own prescribed rituals, prayers, and practices, many Jewish holidays share common features. The Sabbath and the most important Jewish holidays are mandated in the Torah. These holidays are Rosh Hashanah, Yom Kippur, Sukkot and its concluding Eighth Day of Assembly, Passover, and Shavuot. The Torah prescribes rituals for these special days and requires cessation from work. Three of these holidays, Sukkot, Passover, and Shavuot, are pilgrimage festivals, which in ancient times required a visit to the Temple in Jerusalem. According to the Torah, God liberated the Jewish people from slavery in Egypt, gave them His laws on Mount Sinai, and sustained them in the desert before leading them to the Promised Land of Israel. The Exodus from Egypt and its immediate aftermath constitute the central biblical event in the development of the Jewish religion and of the Jewish peoplehood. The three pilgrimage festivals relate directly to the Exodus: Passover celebrates the Exodus itself; Shavuot (the Feast of Weeks) commemorates the giving of the Torah seven weeks later; and the Feast of Sukkot is a remembrance of the temporary dwellings the Jews inhabited during their forty years of wandering after they left Egypt.

Rosh Hashanah, which marks the Jewish New Year, and Yom Kippur, the Day of Atonement, are also mandated by the Torah. Known together as the High Holy Days or Days of Awe, they are a time for reflection, prayer, and self-improvement. On these days, Jews remember God's relationship with the biblical Patriarchs, Abraham, Isaac, and Jacob, and His covenant with their descendants. Rosh Hashanah, like the pilgrimage festivals, is a joyous holiday as well as a solemn one. Yom Kippur is considered the holiest day of the year and Jews fast to comply with the biblical commandment to "afflict their souls."

Each of these Torah-mandated holidays has its own set of rituals and customs. These practices elevate the holidays above everyday life, encourage spending meaningful time with family and the extended Jewish community, and in turn arouse the interest and curiosity of children. Through these ancient customs, these celebrations become vehicles for passing down Jewish tradition to the next generation. On Passover, Jews eat special foods, including unleavened bread and bitter herbs, to recall the bitterness of slavery in Egypt. During Sukkot, they eat their meals in temporary dwellings to remember the wanderings in the desert after the Exodus. On Rosh Hashanah, a ram's horn is sounded to call the congregation to prayer and reflection. These rituals and many others described in the following chapters have developed over the centuries and connect Jews around the globe through common practices.

Sabbath observance is mandated in the Torah and included specifically in the Ten Commandments, which contain the fundamental moral and religious principles of faith. In addition to the cessation of productive work activity, the Jewish Sabbath is a time for families to come together. It is marked by three special meals, blessings over wine and Sabbath bread, prayer service, and readings from the Torah and Prophets in the synagogue.

HISTORIC HOLIDAYS

The remaining festivals—Purim and Chanukah—are not mandated by the Torah. The story of Purim is recounted in great detail in the Book of Esther, which is within the Writings (Ketuvim) of the Tanakh. Purim celebrates the salvation of the Jewish people from the threat of genocide in ancient Persia. Much like a fairy tale, the story has a powerful king, a heroic queen, a sly villain, and a happy ending. The holiday is celebrated with special foods, the reading of the Book of Esther, a special meal, and gifts to friends and the poor.

Chanukah celebrates the extraordinary victory of the Jews over the Syrian-Greek kingdom. The Jews were led by a small group known as the Maccabees, who reconsecrated the holy Temple in Jerusalem. In commemoration of the victory and the discovery of a small supply of consecrated oil that miraculously burned for eight days, Jews celebrate the holiday by lighting a special candelabra. Like Purim and many other Jewish holidays, many of Chanukah's customs and rituals are centered around children and family.

WHAT IS THE OLD TESTAMENT?

Jewish Scripture, often referred to as the "Old Testament," is more properly called *Tanakh*, an acronym for *Torah* (the Pentateuch or Five Books of Moses), *Neviim* (Prophets, such as Samuel, Isaiah, and Jeremiah), and *Ketuvim* (Writings, which includes Proverbs, Song of Songs, and Ruth).

(THE HEBREW CALENDAR)

Jewish holidays are governed by the Jewish calendar, which is based primarily on lunar months. The twelve lunar months are approximately eleven days shorter than the solar calendar of 365 days, so in seven years out of a cycle of nineteen years, an extra month is added. This solar adjustment is necessary so that the holidays remain within their relative season and Passover remains the "Holiday of Spring," as it is sometimes called.

The Torah specifies the date in the Hebrew month for the major holidays, so it is critical to know when each month begins. In ancient times, the month began when

VARIATIONS ON TRADITIONS

There are many local variations of customs and traditions in the celebrations of the Jewish holidays. A major delineation of the Jewish population is between Ashkenazi and Sephardic Jews. In general, Ashkenazi Jews are those whose families originated in Eastern and Central Europe. Sephardic Jews are descendants of Jews from the Iberian Peninsula who were expelled from Spain and Portugal in the fifteenth century. Many Sephardim ultimately settled in North Africa, Turkey, and the Middle East, including Syria, Iraq, and Iran, as well as in communities in Italy and elsewhere. While the core customs, traditions, and rituals of Ashkenazim and Sephardim are similar, there are interesting variations. For example, Sephardic Jews eat rice and certain other foods on Passover that are prohibited to Ashkenazi Jews. On the Sabbath and festivals, many Sephardic congregations read from a Torah scroll that is encased in wood or silver and held upright while Ashkenazi congregations read from a scroll covered in an elegant mantle of silk or velvet and laid flat on a table.

reliable witnesses observed the first crescent of the new moon in Israel. Then they would send messengers to Jewish communities outside the Holy Land. Because those messengers were not always able to reach distant communities quickly, there was some question as to whether the month prior to Passover or Sukkot was twenty-nine or thirty days. In order to avoid doubt, communities in the Diaspora (that is, outside Israel) celebrated the initial day of the holiday (which requires abstention from work) for two days rather than one. This tradition continued after the calendar was regularized by mathematical calculation, rather than visual observation, which explains why holidays are celebrated by Orthodox and Conservative Jews for two days in the Diaspora but just one in Israel; Reform Jews rely on the mathematically determined calendar and celebrate just one day in the Diaspora.

NOURISHING BODY AND SOUL

Jewish celebrations are invariably based on religious traditions, but they have social and community-based aspects as well. The Sabbath and holidays are occasions for gatherings of family and friends, and customs and rituals almost always include participation by children. Of course, no Jewish celebration is complete without food, and almost all Jewish celebrations include a festive meal featuring special foods that often come to stand as a symbol for the day. On the Sabbath, special bread, called challah, has a place of honor at the table. On Rosh Hashanah, sweet honey is served with challah, and Chanukah celebrants feast on oily foods such as crispy potato latkes and sugary jelly doughnuts. While food is not the focus of this little volume, the following chapters will explain the significance of each of these special meals. Hearty appetite!

ROSH HASHANAH

DAYS *of* PRAYER *and* PERSONAL REFLECTION

ROSH HASHANAH

HEBREW NAME Rosh Hashanah (Beginning or Head of the Year).

ALSO KNOWN AS Yom Hazikaron (Day of Remembrance) and Yom Teruah (Day of Shofar Blasts).

WHEN IT'S CELEBRATED Rosh Hashanah is a two-day holiday that begins on the first day of the Hebrew month of Tishrei, which falls in the autumn in the Northern Hemisphere, sometime in September or early October.

WHAT IT'S ALL ABOUT Rosh Hashanah is the Jewish New Year. It is the first of the High Holy Days and inaugurates the Ten Days of Repentance, which conclude with Yom Kippur. While it is a joyous festival, Rosh Hashanah, unlike January 1, is not simply a day of merriment, since it begins a ten-day period of deep reflection. The holiday is celebrated with prayer service in the synagogue, with the repeated sounding of the shofar, with the consumption of special foods around a festive dinner table, and with the symbolic casting away of sin.

SCRIPTURAL SOURCE The holiday is specifically mandated in the Torah, though the Torah never uses the phrase Rosh Hashanah. Instead, the holiday is proclaimed twice, first as a day of rest commemorated with blasts of the shofar (LEVITICUS 23:24), and then as a "holy assembly on which all work is forbidden and a day of blowing the shofar" (NUMBERS 29:1).

THE STORY Rosh Hashanah is a remembrance of God's kingship of the universe and His creation of the world. It is also a time of personal reflection, self-evaluation, repentance, and commitment to improvement.

ROSH HASHANAH AND THE RETURN FROM EXILE

The Temple in Jerusalem was destroyed by the Babylonians in the sixth century B.C.E. After the Persian conquest of Babylon, the Persian kings permitted the Jews to return to Jerusalem and the Land of Israel. The Book of Nehemiah describes the rejuvenation of religious life among the returnees. Ezra, the scribe and priest, and Nehemiah, who were both leaders of the returning exiles, read from the Torah scroll. They proclaimed that, notwithstanding the devastation in Jerusalem, the day of Rosh Hashanah was holy to God and that the people must not mourn or weep. Instead, they should consume festive food and drink (Nehemiah 8:9–10). Jews in subsequent generations continued to celebrate Rosh Hashanah as a joyous holiday as well as a solemn occasion.

RITUALS AND CUSTOMS

In addition to being a celebration of the new year, Rosh Hashanah begins an intense period of self-evaluation and repentance that reaches its climax on Yom Kippur and ends on Hoshana Rabbah at the end of the Sukkot festival.

SELICHOT AND THE TEN DAYS OF REPENTANCE

Beginning on the Saturday night before Rosh Hashanah (or the previous Saturday night if the first day of Rosh Hashanah falls on Monday or Tuesday), and through Yom Kippur, Jewish congregations recite special poems and prayers known as *Selichot* (from the Hebrew word for "forgiveness"). The Selichot encourage self-evaluation as congregants consider the previous year and look toward the next one, and the prayers create a solemn mood conducive to repentance. The period between Rosh Hashanah and Yom Kippur is known as the Ten Days of Repentance. Special prayers are added to the regular service beseeching God's mercy and forgiveness during this period. According to tradition, God's Book of Judgment is opened on Rosh Hashanah, and individual judgments are sealed as Yom Kippur comes to an end.

(THE SHOFAR)

The shofar is central to the holiday of Rosh Hashanah, so much so that the Torah calls it the Day of Shofar Blasts. The shofar is an ancient musical instrument made from the horn of a ram or sheep. Blowing through the horn causes a column of air inside it to vibrate, creating loud blasts. The shofar has great significance in Jewish history: according to Exodus, the shofar sounded when God gave Moses the Ten Commandments. It also sounded while Joshua conquered the city of Jericho, and it was blasted in ancient times to announce the beginning of holidays.

During the service on the day of Rosh Hashanah, unless it falls on the Sabbath, a congregant plays one hundred blasts of the shofar in the synagogue. The service incorporates three distinct sounds, which are played in a variety of groupings over the course of the service:

T'KIAH: A single plain, deep sound, ending abruptly.

SHEVARIM: Three short sounds blown consecutively.

T'RUAH: A series of nine short notes.

The rabbis give two distinct rationales for the shofar service. First, the stirring sound of the shofar serves as a call for introspection and repentance. Indeed, during the morning weekday services for the entire month preceding Rosh Hashanah, the shofar is sounded to awaken the congregants to the coming holy days. The second and more obscure rationale is that the shofar is a remembrance of Abraham's willingness to sacrifice his son, Isaac, and the substitution at the last moment of a ram for the child. In this rationale, the shofar serves as a testament of the

Jewish people's devotion to God's commandments and its readiness to bear the burdens of faith.

TASHLICH

On the afternoon of the first day of Rosh Hashanah (or the second day if the first day is the Sabbath), Jews gather at a body of water such as a seashore, bank of a river, or lake, and symbolically cast their sins away in a ritual called *Tashlich* in Hebrew, or "casting off." This ancient custom probably derives from the passage in Micah 7:19: "He [God] will cast all of our sins into the depths of the sea." In addition to reciting prayers and psalms, many throw breadcrumbs or small stones into the water to dramatize the casting away of sin. Nine days after Rosh Hashanah, on Yom Kippur, water again plays a prominent role in encouraging repentance. The Book of Jonah, which is read in the afternoon on Yom Kippur, tells the story of the prophet who went to sea in order to escape God's commandment to warn the sinners of Nineveh. Jonah was swallowed by a great fish who delivered him to the shore so that he could fulfill his mission, and the sinners repented.

(FESTIVE FOODS)

The Rosh Hashanah evening dinner is a major family event, and the festive dinner table includes special foods that play a part in celebrating the occasion. Round, braided challahs (holiday loaves of bread) sweetened with raisins are served, rather than the traditional rectangular or oval challahs, to symbolize the cycle of the year. After the blessing of the challah, pieces are dipped in honey and served to everyone at the table, along with honey-dipped apples, to denote the hope for a sweet year. Many also have the custom of displaying the head of a fish on the table, a reference to the head of the year. Other special foods on the table may include spinach, beets, and dates, which grow in profusion in Israel and are symbolic of prosperity, as well as pomegranates, whose many seeds exemplify fruitfulness. When the special foods are consumed, various requests to God are recited. These requests contain wordplay connecting the food with the request. For example, while consuming beets, diners offer a request that God vanquish our enemies. *Selek*, the Hebrew word for "beets," is a homonym for a word meaning "to banish."

SELECTED QUOTATIONS

On proclaiming the holiday: *"The Lord spoke to Moses, saying: Speak to the Children of Israel and proclaim that the first day of the seventh month shall be a day of rest, commemorated with blasts of the shofar."*
—LEVITICUS 23:23–24

A key prayer, recited three times each day during the period between Rosh Hashanah and Yom Kippur: *"Remember us for life, O King who wishes life, and inscribe us in the Book of Life, for your sake, O King of life."*
—PART OF THE AMIDAH (STANDING PRAYER) SERVICE

On the symbolic casting away of sin: *"Who is like you, God, who pardons sin and forgives iniquity of the remnant of his heritage?"*
—OPENING LINE OF THE TASHLICH SERVICE

IMPORTANT WORDS AND PHRASES

MACHZOR: A prayer book specifically for the holiday service.

SHANA TOVA, L'SHANA TOVA TIKATEVU, and SHANA TOVA UMETUKAH: New Year greetings meaning, respectively, "A good year," "May you be inscribed for a good year," and "A good, sweet year."

SHOFAR: A ram's horn sounded as part of the Rosh Hashanah prayer service.

TASHLICH: The ceremony performed at a body of water to symbolically cast away sin.

TESHUVAH: Repentance, the primary commitment undertaken during the High Holy Days of Rosh Hashanah and Yom Kippur.

YOM KIPPUR

A DAY of PRAYER and REPENTANCE

HEBREW NAME Yom Kippur or Yom Kippurim (Day of Repentance).

ALSO KNOWN AS The Sabbath of Sabbaths, the Day of Atonement, and the Day of Judgment.

WHEN IT'S CELEBRATED Yom Kippur is observed on the tenth day of the Hebrew month of Tishrei, nine days after the first day of Rosh Hashanah. Yom Kippur always falls in September or October.

WHAT IT'S ALL ABOUT Yom Kippur is the holiest day of the Jewish year, which is why it is called the "Sabbath of Sabbaths." It is the culmination of the Ten Days of Repentance that begins on Rosh Hashanah. The day is marked by fasting and prayer service in the synagogue. The central themes of the day are repentance by individuals and the community and prayers for atonement.

SCRIPTURAL SOURCE There are three scriptural references to Yom Kippur in the Torah:

Leviticus 16:29–34 proclaims the holiday for all time as one in which Jews are to "afflict" their souls and cease from all work, and as a day on which the entire community atones for its sins. Leviticus 23:26–32 and Numbers 29:7–11 repeat the prohibition of work and the requirement of afflicting the soul for repentance.

THE STORY In ancient times, when the Temple in Jerusalem stood, the High Priest performed sacrifices and rituals unique to Yom Kippur seeking forgiveness from God for the sins of the people. It was only on this day that the High Priest was permitted to enter the Holy of Holies, the innermost section of the Temple where the presence of God was felt more strongly than anywhere else on earth. Subsequent to the destruction of the Temple and the elimination of sacrifices and the role of the High Priest, prayer has replaced sacrifices and Jews continue to seek forgiveness and mercy through fasting.

RITUALS AND CUSTOMS

The rituals and customs surrounding Yom Kippur are designed to foster self-evaluation and repentance.

AFFLICTING THE SOUL

T he Torah commands that one must "afflict the soul" on Yom Kippur, which has come to involve fasting and the denial of other bodily comforts. The fast of Yom Kippur begins shortly before sunset on the evening before the day and lasts for twenty-five hours until nightfall on Yom Kippur. In addition to fasting, observant Jews refrain from wearing leather shoes and washing their entire body, and women refrain from using makeup and perfume.

FESTIVE MEALS

A lthough Yom Kippur is a holy and solemn day, it is also considered a festival, albeit one with special rules. Every Jewish festival has a holiday meal, and Yom Kippur is no exception. The Yom Kippur festive meal takes place right before the fast begins, and many families also celebrate the end of the fast with a break-the-fast meal with friends.

THE YOM KIPPUR SERVICES

Y om Kippur is widely observed by secular as well as religious Jews. Synagogue attendance is widespread and far exceeds that of the weekly Sabbath service. Jews attend the synagogue on Yom Kippur eve for the special Kol Nidre service and also during the day itself.

KOL NIDRE The service on Yom Kippur eve begins with the solemn recitation of Kol Nidre, which means "all vows." Kol Nidre is not actually a prayer but a declaration in the ancient Aramaic language that all personal vows that may be made in the coming year are to be considered null and void and not binding on the person making them. The vows referred to in Kol Nidre relate only to personal undertakings (such as fasting and performing certain good deeds) that have no bearing on other persons or interests; the prayer does not relate to obligations undertaken to others or to testimony in legal cases. The Kol Nidre declaration is recited three times by the cantor in a moving, ancient melody with increasing intensity and volume each time. Although the Kol Nidre declaration consists of dry and legalistic phrases, because of its solemnity and haunting melody, it has achieved a significance beyond the words themselves.

THE DAYTIME SERVICE The synagogue service on Yom Kippur day, which is much longer than any other service, is centered on repentance and confession of sin. The traditional holiday prayer book, called the *machzor*, contains formulaic prayers and confessions that are recited both silently and aloud. Congregants are also encouraged to engage in self-reflection and personal repentance. In the afternoon service, the cantor and congregation recall the Yom Kippur service and sacrifices performed by the High Priest in the Temple in Jerusalem. Later in the afternoon, the biblical Book of Jonah is read.

NE'ILAH The last part of the Yom Kippur service consists of the special prayers of Ne'ilah, which means "closing," a reference to the closing of the Temple gates at the end of the ancient service. It also refers to the symbolic "closing" of the Gates of Heaven at the end of the Ten Days of Repentance. According to Jewish tradition, the Book of Judgment is opened on Rosh Hashanah and sealed at the conclusion of Ne'ilah, so the congregation prays during the service to be "sealed" in the Book of Life. At the conclusion of Ne'ilah, a single blast of the shofar is sounded to mark the end of the Holy Day.

ATTIRE On Yom Kippur, congregants dress as they would on any other holiday in dignified and festive clothing, but many men and women wear white clothing to signify purity, as well as non-leather shoes like sneakers or sandals.

THE BOOK OF JONAH Jonah was a biblical prophet who lived in the north of Israel. He was commanded by God to warn the inhabitants of Nineveh, a large Assyrian city (today in Iraq), that their city would be destroyed because of their sins. Jonah, in defiance of the commandment, fled by sea in another direction. God caused a storm on the sea, and the sailors, realizing that the storm was caused by Jonah's presence, cast him into the deep. A great fish swallowed Jonah, who survived for three days in its belly, where he repented of his actions. The great fish deposited Jonah near Nineveh and Jonah warned the inhabitants. The citizens of Nineveh, led by their ruler, repented, and God spared the city. The Book of Jonah is read on Yom Kippur to demonstrate God's willingness to forgive those who, like the residents of the ancient city of Nineveh, are prepared to repent.

SELECTED QUOTATIONS

On proclaiming the holiday: *"And it shall be for you a law forever, in the seventh month, on the tenth day, you shall afflict your souls and you shall do no work. . . . For on this day, atonement shall be made for you to purify you; from all your sins you shall be cleansed before God."*
—LEVITICUS 16:29–30

From the words of the Kol Nidre service: *"All vows, prohibitions, oaths . . . that we may swear upon ourselves from this Yom Kippur until the next Yom Kippur . . . We regret them and they shall be null and void and without power . . . "*

God's reaction to the repentance of the people of Nineveh: *"And God saw their deeds, how they repented from their evil ways. And God relented from the punishment He had planned to bring upon them."*
—JONAH 3:10

IMPORTANT WORDS AND PHRASES

KETIVAH V'CHATIMA TOVAH: Traditional Yom Kippur greeting wishing one a good judgment, written and sealed for a sweet year.

KOL NIDRE: The declaration of nullification of future vows recited on Yom Kippur eve.

NE'ILAH: The concluding service on Yom Kippur, when the Gates of Judgment are "closed."

T'KIAH GEDOLA: The single shofar blast that signifies the end of Yom Kippur.

SUKKOT

LIFE *in a*
TEMPORARY DWELLING

SUKKOT

HEBREW NAME Sukkot (meaning "booths" or "tabernacles").

ALSO KNOWN AS The Festival of Ingathering of Crops and the Festival of the Lord.

WHEN IT'S CELEBRATED Sukkot begins on the fifteenth day of the Hebrew month of Tishrei, two weeks after Rosh Hashanah, five days after Yom Kippur, and six months after Passover; like Passover, Sukkot begins on a full moon.

WHAT IT'S ALL ABOUT Sukkot is a seven-day festival during which meals are eaten in a *sukkah*, a temporary dwelling built outside the home. On each day of the festival, a blessing is recited over four plant species mandated especially for the holiday. Sukkot is followed immediately by Shemini Atzeret and Simchat Torah, which close the holiday season. The sukkah and the four species are once-a-year customs and excite curiosity among children and adults alike. Like the Passover seder, the Sukkot customs and rituals are vehicles to transmit Jewish tradition.

SCRIPTURAL SOURCE The festival is mentioned several times in the Torah. The most detailed reference is in Leviticus 23:39–42: "When you gather the fruits of the land, celebrate the Festival of the Lord." The Bible proclaims a seven-day holiday with an additional eighth day of celebration and assembly. Work is prohibited on the first and last day, and Jews are instructed to take four species—a special fruit, branches of palm trees, boughs of leafy trees, and willows of the brook—and rejoice before God. During the festival, Jews have traditionally lived in booths for seven days in order to commemorate the temporary dwellings of Jews during their wanderings after the Exodus from Egypt.

THE STORY There are two distinct themes to the Festival of Sukkot. The first, and the one that gives the holiday its name, is a remembrance of the Exodus and the hardships sustained by the Jews in their forty years of wandering in the desert. God proclaims the holiday and the requirement to live in booths for seven days so that "your generations will know that I made the Children of Israel dwell in booths when I took them out of Egypt." The second theme is the commemoration of an agricultural celebration at the time of the gathering of the crops and the close of the yearly agricultural cycle. To that end, a ritual is enacted with four distinct species of plant life.

RITUALS AND CUSTOMS

The rituals and customs of Sukkot reflect the two themes of the holiday. Families eat their meals in a temporary dwelling, the sukkah, in commemoration of the fragile shelters in which the Jews lived in their desert wanderings. Jews also recognize the agricultural aspect of the holiday and perform a special ritual with four agricultural species.

THE SUKKAH

J̌ ust as the seder has come to epitomize the Passover ritual, the sukkah is the principal symbol of the Sukkot holiday. The sukkah must be a temporary dwelling created expressly for the holiday to reflect the temporary nature of the "homes" Jews lived in while wandering in the desert. The sukkah must have a roof made of organic materials (known as *s'chach*) such as palm leaves, bamboo poles, or pine boards, and must not have four full permanent walls, to reflect the temporary nature of the dwelling. Families and synagogues usually build their *sukkot* (the plural of sukkah, as well as the name of the holiday) immediately after Yom Kippur and deconstruct it immediately after the holiday. The sukkah is usually beautified and decorated with hanging fruits, wall coverings, and other adornments to make the structure a comfortable and welcoming space. The requirement to "live" in the sukkah is generally interpreted to mean "eat" in the sukkah, although some do sleep in the sukkah as well. A special blessing is made in the sukkah before each meal.

RECITING THE USHPIZIN In the sukkah, some Jews have the custom to each day recite the Ushpizin, the word for "guests" in Aramaic. This short recital symbolically welcomes heroes of Israel into the sukkah: Abraham, Isaac, Jacob, Joseph, Moses, Aaron, and David. In recent years, some have also welcomed heroines including Sarah, Rebecca, Rachel, Leah, Miriam, Deborah, and Esther.

THE FOUR SPECIES

The Torah stipulates that Jews are required to take four specific species of plant life on the holiday and rejoice before God, in thanksgiving for the harvest that has just been reaped. In practice, the four species are:

ARAVAH: Willow stalks.

ETROG: A citrus fruit known as the citron, which is similar in appearance to a lemon.

HADAS: Myrtle branches.

LULAV: A frond of a date palm tree.

The date palm frond, myrtle branches, and willow stalks are artfully bound together with dried palm leaves in a tall sticklike formation. Each day of the festival, celebrants hold this combination of species along with the etrog and make a special blessing. The blessing refers specifically to the lulav (the date palm frond) but encompasses all four species. In the synagogue, the four species are also held and waved together when certain psalms are

recited in the morning service. Children particularly love this ritual since they can sway and shake the lulav to their hearts' content.

HOSHANA RABBAH

The seventh day of Sukkot is known as Hoshana Rabbah, the "Great Supplication." In the morning service of that day, congregants carrying the four species parade

WHAT FRUIT IS THE ETROG?

The Torah does not specify that the etrog should be a citron—rather it refers to the etrog only as the fruit of a good (or beautiful) tree—though it is universally accepted as the citron. The citron has very little value for fifty-one weeks of the year, but before the holiday of Sukkot, the price of an unblemished fruit rises, and it is a common sight, in Jewish neighborhoods, to see people minutely examine citrons in order to pick a beautiful, unblemished one. Many Jews find uses for the etrog once the holiday is over by making jams or liqueurs, or by placing cloves in it and using it as the spice smelled at the end of Shabbat.

READING ECCLESIASTES On the Sabbath that falls within Sukkot, the Book of Ecclesiastes is read aloud in the synagogue. Ecclesiastes is a solemn text that reminds the listener of the challenges and futility of life, and includes the well-known phrase "Vanity of vanities, all is vanity." This somberness appears out of character with Sukkot, a joyful holiday when Jews are commanded to rejoice. However, reading the Book of Ecclesiastes reminds the listener to keep everything in perspective, with all things in moderation.

around the synagogue seven times while reciting prayers of praise and gratitude. This unusual ritual is reminiscent of the service in the Temple on the holiday of Sukkot. At the conclusion of the seventh circuit, it is customary to beat a bundle of willows on the ground, symbolizing the casting away of sin. Hoshana Rabbah is considered the final end of the Days of Awe, which begin on Rosh Hashanah and reach their climax on Yom Kippur.

SELECTED QUOTATIONS

On proclaiming the holiday: *"But, on the fifteenth day of the seventh month, when you gather the fruits of the land, celebrate the Festival of the Lord for seven days. . . . And you shall take a fruit of a goodly tree, branches of a palm tree, boughs of a thick tree, and willows of the brook, and you shall rejoice before the Lord your God for seven days. . . . You shall dwell in booths for seven days, all the citizens in Israel shall dwell in booths so that your generations shall know that I caused the Children of Israel to dwell in booths when I took them out of Egypt."*
—LEVITICUS 23:39–42

The blessings on the four species: *"Blessed are You, O Lord our God, King of the universe, who sanctified us and commanded us concerning the taking of the palm frond. Blessed are You, O Lord our God, King of the universe, who has kept us alive, sustained us, and brought us to this time."*

On the vanity of man, from the reading on Shabbat during Sukkot: *"There is nothing new beneath the sun."*
—ECCLESIASTES 1:9

On rejoicing on the holiday of Sukkot: *"You shall make the festival of Sukkot for seven days when you have gathered from the threshing floor and wine press. And you shall rejoice in your holiday, you, and your son and your daughter, and your servant and your maid . . . and you shall be altogether joyful."*

—DEUTERONOMY 16:13–16

IMPORTANT WORDS AND PHRASES

ETROG: The citron fruit, which is the most prominent of the four species used on Sukkot to fulfill the biblical commandment.

LULAV: The palm frond bundled with willow and myrtle and held with the etrog.

S'CHACH: The roof of the sukkah, made of organic material, such as palm fronds or bamboo poles.

SUKKAH: A temporary outdoor dwelling in which Jews take their meals during the holiday of Sukkot.

SHEMINI ATZERET & SIMCHAT TORAH

THE END *of the* HOLIDAY SEASON

SHEMINI ATZERET
&
SIMCHAT TORAH

HEBREW NAME Shemini Atzeret (Eighth Day of Assembly) and Simchat Torah (Rejoicing with the Law).

WHEN IT'S CELEBRATED The holiday begins on the twenty-second day of the month of Tishrei, immediately after the seven days of Sukkot.

WHAT IT'S ALL ABOUT There are two distinct aspects to the holiday of Shemini Atzeret and Simchat Torah. It is both a farewell to the holiday season and a time of great joy as the Torah cycle is concluded and begun again. These days are combined in Israel, as well as in the Reform and Reconstructionist movements, and are two separate holy days elsewhere in the Diaspora. The days mark the conclusion of the Sukkot holiday and the completion of the Torah, which is accompanied by joyous dancing and singing.

THE STORY Shemini Atzeret, the Eighth Day of Assembly, immediately follows the seven days of Sukkot. It is technically a separate holiday and not part of Sukkot, and there is no requirement to dwell in a sukkah or pray with the four species, but because it follows Sukkot without a break, many consider this day a continuation of Sukkot. The Torah commands that this Eighth Day should be a day of solemn assembly, closing the long holiday period that began three weeks earlier on Rosh Hashanah. Talmudic literature views it as an opportunity for God and the Jewish people to bid the holidays farewell together.

Simchat Torah (whether combined with Shemini Atzeret or celebrated separately) is a time of great celebration. On that day, the year's cycle of weekly Torah portions comes to an end with the final words of Deuteronomy; it is immediately followed with a reading from the beginning, Genesis chapter 1. The day is marked with joyous (and sometimes boisterous) dancing in the synagogue and is a fitting end to the month of holidays.

RITUALS AND CUSTOMS

Simchat Torah, as its name denotes, is a time of rejoicing with the Torah. There are two main rituals on the holiday, both pertaining to the Torah itself.

HAKAFOT

On the eve of Simchat Torah, the synagogue is a scene of great joy and dancing. The congregants are called up to the front of the synagogue to receive *hakafot* (Hebrew for "circuits"). With Torahs in hand, congregants dance around the synagogue and often in the streets as well. Seven hakafot are performed, and each member of the community is given a chance to dance with a Torah. While parading with the Torahs and making a circuit of the synagogue, the worshipers chant biblical and poetic verses. The hakafot begin with the verse: "Please God, save us; please God, bring us success; please God, answer us on the day we call you." In many congregations, hakafot are repeated during the morning service on Simchat Torah. Children often participate enthusiastically in the Hakafot service by dancing with the grownups carrying the Torahs, and they are sometimes given paper flags and candied apples.

COMPLETING THE TORAH AND STARTING AGAIN

In the morning service, the last Torah portion (*parashah* in Hebrew) from Deuteronomy is read. It is Moses's final blessing to the Jewish people and includes the poignant episode of Moses's death. It is a short parashah, and it is read repeatedly so that every congregant can be called to the Torah to read a blessing over it. When the reading is completed, another Torah is taken from the ark, an honored person is called up, and the reader begins the Torah again from Genesis. The message to the community is that Torah study is never complete: when one comes to the end, one begins again.

SELECTED QUOTATIONS

On the name of the holiday: *"On the eighth day, you shall have a solemn assembly, you shall not do any manner of work."*
—NUMBERS 29:35

After the dedication of the Temple by King Solomon: *"On the eighth day, he [Solomon] sent the people away and they blessed the King and they went to their tents happy and content with all the good that God had done for David [Solomon's father], His servant, and Israel, His people."*
—I KINGS 8:66

Rabbinic concept expressing God's regret on departing after a month of holidays: *Kashe alai pridatchem* ("It is difficult for me to separate from you").

IMPORTANT WORDS AND PHRASES

ALIYAH: The call to the Torah to say the blessing over the reading.

HAKAFOT: The circuits of the synagogue while dancing with the Torah on Simchat Torah.

CHANUKAH

A FESTIVAL of LIGHTS

CHANUKAH

HEBREW NAME Chanukah (from the Hebrew word meaning "dedication").

ALSO KNOWN AS The Festival of Lights and the Festival of Dedication. The holiday name is sometimes spelled Hanukah, Hanukkah, or Hanuka.

WHEN IT'S CELEBRATED Chanukah begins on the twenty-fifth day of the Hebrew month of Kislev, which occurs in late November or December.

WHAT IT'S ALL ABOUT Chanukah is an eight-day festival commemorating the rededication of the Second Holy Temple after the successful Maccabean revolt against the Syrian-Greeks. It is an enchanting holiday celebrated with the lighting of a special candelabrum called the meno-rah or *chanukiah*, which has nine branches. The holiday is also celebrated with special foods and games and with the giving of gifts. In the Diaspora, and particularly in the United States, Chanukah is sometimes treated as a winter festival parallel to Christmas.

SCRIPTURAL SOURCES There is no scriptural source for Chanukah since the events celebrated took place after the closing of the Jewish canon. Much of the Chanukah story is portrayed in the late second-century B.C.E. books Maccabees I and Maccabees II, which are included in the Christian canon of various churches, including the Roman Catholic Church, but not in the Jewish canon. During the first century C.E., the historian Flavius Josephus, in *Antiquities of the Jews*, described the establishment of Chanukah by the Maccabees in the second century B.C.E. The Chanukah story is embellished and laws are set out in the Talmud, codified around 500 C.E.

THE STORY The story of Chanukah centers around two wondrous miracles. The first, a military victory of a relatively small people (the Jews) over the powerful Seleucid Empire, is documented by nearly contemporaneous historical accounts. The second miracle, that a small container with one day's supply of oil lasted for eight days, lacks contemporaneous historical evidence but has come to be the focus of the holiday.

Alexander the Great conquered the Middle East during his wars against the Persians around 330 B.C.E. Subsequent to his death, Alexander's kingdom was divided into subkingdoms. After a period of conflict, around the year 200 B.C.E., the Land of Israel became subject to the Seleucid-Greek Empire centered in Syria. At first, the conquerors were tolerant of the Jewish religion, but around 170 B.C.E., the Seleucid monarch Antiochus IV invaded Israel and defiled the Temple in Jerusalem by building an altar to the pagan god Zeus. Antiochus sought to outlaw and destroy Judaism by forbidding circumcision and prohibiting the practice of the religion. These actions brought on a revolt in Israel led by Mattityahu, a Jewish priest, and his five sons. Judah, foremost among them, was called Judah the Maccabee, meaning "Judah the Hammer," for his forceful actions against the Seleucid Greeks. After several years of battles, Judah and his brothers (now collectively known as Maccabees) were successful in expelling the Seleucid Greeks. The Maccabees cleansed the Jewish Temple in Jerusalem, built a new altar, and created new holy vessels.

The story told in Maccabees I ends with the rededication of the Temple, an eight-day celebration, and the institution by Judah Maccabee and his brothers of the holiday of Chanukah, to be celebrated throughout the ages.

A second miracle has been incorporated into this miraculous military victory. The Talmud and later Jewish books tell that in the course of rededicating the Temple, a single container of oil was found, which was sufficient to light the menorah in the Temple for just one day. Amazingly, the small quantity of olive oil lasted eight days, so that the menorah could be lit each evening as required.

RITUALS AND CUSTOMS

Chanukah is known as the festival of lights, and the principal ritual of the holiday is the lighting of the menorah. It is an especially joyful time for children, as they delight in games and receiving gifts.

LIGHTING THE MENORAH

The principal and defining ritual of Chanukah is the lighting of the menorah on each of the eight nights of the holiday. Families tend to light the candles together, and many consider lighting the menorah a cherished family occasion. The Chanukah menorah is lit to recollect the rededication of the Temple when the Temple Menorah was relit, and also to commemorate the miracle of the container of oil that burned for eight days rather than one.

The Chanukah menorah, also called the chanukiah, has eight equally sized branches for candles plus an additional distinctive branch called the *shamash*, which is used to light the other candles. On the first night of Chanukah,

> **THE MENORAH** The ancient menorah used
> in the Temple in Jerusalem is described in the Bible
> in great detail (EXODUS 25:31–40). It had seven lamps
> and consisted of a shaft and six branches. As man-
> dated by the Bible (EXODUS 27:21), the lamps of the
> menorah were lit daily in the evening with specially
> consecrated olive oil. A representation of the Sec-
> ond Temple menorah is found on the Arch of Titus in
> Rome, celebrating the Roman victory over the Jews
> in the Judean revolt of 70 C.E.

one candle is lit; on the second night, two candles, and
so on until the eighth night when the shamash is used to
light all eight candles.

Before the candles are lit, three blessings are recited
over the Chanukah menorah on the first night of Chanukah and two on each subsequent night. The blessings
relate to the commandment to light the menorah, to recall
the miracles that took place in ancient time, and to give
thanks for living to see the holiday.

After the candles are lit, two hymns are traditionally sung. The first, "Hanerot Halalu" ("These Candles"),

recalls the miracles of Chanukah, and the second, the six-stanza "Maoz Tzur" ("Stronghold of the Rock," meaning God), recalls various episodes of salvation among the Jewish people.

CHANUKAH GAMES

L̲ike many Jewish holidays, Chanukah encourages children to participate in the celebration by engaging them with games and gifts.

The dreidel (Yiddish from the word that means "spin") is a four-sided top with Hebrew letters on each side (*nun*, *gimel*, *hey*, and *shin*, the Hebrew equivalents of *n*, *g*, *h*, and *s*). The letters correspond to the first letters of the four words that reflect one of the Chanukah mottos: *Nes gadol hayah sham*, "A great miracle happened there." In Israel, the dreidel is called a *sevivon* (modern Hebrew for "spinner"). The letter *shin* for *sham* (meaning "there") is changed to *pei* for *po* (meaning "here"), so the motto becomes "A great miracle happened here." The dreidel game is a mild form of gambling, with players taking turns spinning and putting money in or taking money out of the "pot," depending on the letter spun.

GIVING GIFTS

It's become a tradition for family members to give gifts on Chanukah. Chanukah *gelt* (Yiddish for "money") is typically coins given by parents and grandparents to children. In recent times, various chocolatiers have created chocolate coins covered in gold and silver foil to be distributed as Chanukah gelt.

FESTIVE FOODS

It's customary to eat foods that are fried in oil on Chanukah to recall the miracle of the long-lasting container of oil. Potato pancakes, called latkes, are the quintessential Chanukah food. In recent years, and particularly in Israel, jelly doughnuts have also become a popular fried holiday food.

SELECTED QUOTATIONS

On proclaiming the holiday of Chanukah: *"Moreover Judah [the Maccabee] and his brothers with the whole congregation of Israel ordained that the days of the dedication of the altar should be kept in their season from year to year for eight days."*
—I MACCABEES 4:59

From a special addition to the daily prayer on Chanukah: *"In the days of the Hasmonean, Mattityahu, the son of Yochanan, High Priest, when the wicked kingdom of Greece rose up against your people [Israel] to make them forget the Torah and to cause them to transgress your laws. . . . You stood for them in their time of distress, fought their battles, defended their rights and avenged their wrongs, delivered the strong to the hands of the weak, the many to the few, and the evil to the righteous."*

The opening line of "Maoz Tzur": *"Strong rock of my salvation, I delight in singing your praises."*

IMPORTANT WORDS AND PHRASES

CHANUKAH GELT: Gifts of money or chocolate coins given to children on Chanukah.

CHANUKIAH: Hebrew word for the nine-branch menorah.

DREIDEL: The Chanukah toy that is similar to a top, with letters on each of its four sides.

LATKES: A traditional Chanukah food, latkes are pancakes, usually made of grated potatoes, fried in oil.

MACCABEE: The name, meaning "hammer," given to the sons of Mattityahu who battled and defeated the Greeks.

"MAOZ TZUR": The hymn meaning "Stronghold of the Rock," sung after lighting the Chanukah candles to celebrate incidents of salvation.

MENORAH: The candelabrum with nine branches (including one shamash) lit on each of the nights of Chanukah.

NES GADOL HAYAH SHAM: "A great miracle happened there," a motto of Chanukah; the first letters in Hebrew are inscribed on the four sides of the dreidel.

SHAMASH: The candle in the special ninth branch of the Chanukah menorah used to light the other candles.

PURIM

A FUN-FILLED CELEBRATION *of* TRIUMPH OVER OUR ENEMIES

HEBREW NAME Purim (meaning "lots," as in drawing lots in a lottery).

WHEN IT'S CELEBRATED Purim falls in the late winter or early spring, on the fourteenth day of the Hebrew month of Adar (Adar II in a leap year), which is one month before Passover.

WHAT IT'S ALL ABOUT Purim is a joyous and whimsical holiday that celebrates the deliverance of the Jews in the fifth century B.C.E. from the murderous schemes of Haman, the grand vizier of the Persian king Ahasuerus. Jews throughout the world celebrate Purim by having fun: children (and often adults) dress up in all manner of costumes, and adults participate in community-sponsored satirical plays called Purimspiels. The Book of Esther is read in the synagogue and a festive meal is shared with family and friends. Gifts of special foods are delivered to neighbors and friends, and charity is given to those in need.

SCRIPTURAL SOURCE The biblical Book of Esther.

THE STORY The story of Purim is a riveting and triumphant account of personal and communal strength. The tale is recounted in novella form in the Book of Esther, which is known as Megillat Esther or the Megillah.

In the sixth century B.C.E., the Jews were exiled from their homeland by Nebuchadnezzar, the king of

THE BOOK OF ESTHER The Book of Esther was the last book of the Tanakh (the Hebrew Bible) to be canonized. It is one of only two books in the Tanakh that does not mention God's name (the other being the Song of Songs). It is also the only book in the Tanakh not found in whole or in part in the Dead Sea Scrolls.

neo-Babylon. As a result of the Persian conquest of Babylon, the Jews were scattered throughout the Persian Empire, including the capital of Shushan (Susa). The Purim story begins with a six-month-long celebration given by Persian king Ahasuerus for his princes and servants. This festival was followed by a seven-day party in the capital. At the end of the party, the king called for his wife, Queen Vashti, so he could show off her beauty to the assembled crowd of princes and commoners. Vashti refused to show herself, and the king dismissed her as queen.

WHO WAS AHASUERUS? Scholars seem to be divided between Artaxerxes II (ruled 405–359 B.C.E.) and Xerxes I (ruled 486–465 B.C.E.). There is no clear consensus, and ancient sources, including Josephus (first century C.E.), seem to favor the former. There do not appear to be any corroborating histories of the Esther-Mordecai-Haman story.

The king then ordered that all young women in the kingdom be presented so that he could choose a new queen. The king favored Esther, a Jewish girl (whose Hebrew name was Hadassah) who was being raised in Shushan by her uncle Mordecai. Following her uncle's instruction, Esther did not tell the king that she was Jewish. Mordecai proved himself useful almost immediately by uncovering a plot against the king's life. The conspirators were executed, and Mordecai's deeds were recorded in the king's Book of Chronicles.

At this point in the story, the villainous Haman appears, a courtier appointed by King Ahasuerus as grand vizier. Haman instructed all residents of the empire to bow down before him, but Mordecai refused to do so. Haman was so infuriated that he plotted to kill not just Mordecai but all Jews throughout the Persian kingdom. Haman obtained the king's permission to proceed with his plans, and Haman conducted a lottery of months and days, settling on the thirteenth day of Adar as the date for the destruction of the Jews. When Mordecai learned of the impending threat, he ordered his fellow Jews to engage in fasting and acts of penitence. Esther, hoping to get the king to reverse this ruling, asked the king to come along with Haman to a private banquet that she planned for the next day.

Haman and the king went to Esther's banquet at which Esther asked the two men to come to a second feast on the next day. When Haman left the first banquet, he again encountered Mordecai, who once again refused to bow down to him. Haman was so enraged that he had a gallows built from which to hang Mordecai the next day. That very night, the king, suffering from insomnia, had his Book of Chronicles read to him and learned that Mordecai was not rewarded for saving the king from the assassins' plot. Just then, Haman appeared in the courtyard. The king, who wanted to reward someone in his favor, asked Haman for his advice. Haman, thinking the king meant himself, suggested that the honoree be dressed in the king's clothes and be placed on the king's horse led by a courtier who shouts: "Thus shall be done to a man whom the king favors." To his horror, Haman is instructed to honor Mordecai in that fashion.

JEWISH AND SECULAR NAMES

The practice of giving Jewish children names common to the country they inhabit as well as Hebrew names is an ancient one. Today Esther and Mordecai are perfectly fine Jewish and Hebrew names. They actually derive from Persian deities, Astarte and Marduk. We know that Esther's Hebrew name was Hadassah; we don't know if Mordecai had a different Hebrew name. Today, throughout the world, except in Israel, Jewish children are usually given both Hebrew and secular names, which are sometimes, but not necessarily, related.

That evening, at Esther's second banquet, Esther revealed that Haman intended to kill all the Jews, including herself and, as one of the king's ministers advised, also Mordecai, who had saved the king. The king then ordered Haman's execution on the gallows prepared for Mordecai. The king's order of extermination previously given to Haman was not subject to countermand, so the king allowed a second order permitting the Jews to defend themselves and preemptively attack their enemies. On the thirteenth of Adar, the date prepared for their destruction, the Jews rose up and killed 75,000 of their enemies. The king appointed Mordecai as his second in command, and Mordecai decreed that the fourteenth of Adar should, in perpetuity, be a day of feasting and rejoicing among the Jews in all the lands they inhabit.

RITUALS AND CUSTOMS

On Purim, the Book of Esther is read in the synagogue and children and adults alike engage in playful activities and share gifts of delicacies.

FAST OF ESTHER

Prior to Purim on the thirteenth of Adar, Jews observe a fast called Taanit Esther, or Fast of Esther, in commemoration of Esther's three-day fast before she went to see the king in order to save her life and the lives of her people. After the fast concludes, the holiday officially starts.

T here are four ritually mandated components in the proper celebration of Purim:

READING THE BOOK OF ESTHER The Book of Esther is read both evening and morning in the synagogue. It is chanted with a special tune and, in most synagogues, children are encouraged to make noise (with noisemakers called *groggers* or otherwise) in order to blot out Haman's name when it is read in the text.

CHARITY As commanded by Mordecai and Esther, one must give gifts of charity to the poor. Most synagogues have special collection plates that are used to fulfill this mitzvah.

PURIM BASKETS In order to spread the joy of the holiday, one must present gifts of at least two types of food called *mishloach manot* (literally, "the sending of portions") to at least two friends or neighbors. In Jewish neighborhoods on Purim, it is quite common to see individuals or families scurrying around to give these gifts.

FEAST OF PURIM One must partake in a festive meal known as Seudat Purim (the Feast of Purim) or simply as the seudah. Families usually have this feast at home, but many synagogues sponsor a community seudah.

(FESTIVE CUSTOMS)

I n addition to the ritually mandated components of Purim, many Jews observe Purim in other celebratory ways.

CHILDREN'S CELEBRATIONS Children dress up in various costumes, not necessarily related to Purim. It is common to see some children dressed as Queen Esther and other children as Superman. The object is simply to have fun. Many Jewish communities have a children's carnival on Purim with games and refreshments.

ADULT CELEBRATIONS Purim is the one day in the year on which frivolity replaces the usually serious nature of religious life, and alcoholic beverages tend to be a part of adult celebrations. Many Jewish communities and synagogue groups stage satiric performances, called Purimspiels, in which religious and lay members participate. These plays are usually only lightly related to the Esther story and are likely to poke fun at contemporary events and personalities. It is common to see the community rabbi dressed in an outlandish costume participating in the festivities.

FESTIVE FOODS Among Ashkenazim, the most famous Purim specialties are hamantaschen (literally translated as "Haman's pockets"), triangular pastries filled with fruit preserves that evoke the hat or pocket Haman wore; similarly, Sephardim eat fazuelos, fried pastries.

(SHUSHAN PURIM)

S hushan Purim, the fifteenth day of Adar (one day after Purim), is the day on which the holiday is actually celebrated in Jerusalem and in other ancient walled cities. During the actual Purim events, the Jews of Shushan needed both the thirteenth and fourteenth of Adar to overcome their enemies, so the holiday was celebrated on the fifteenth.

SELECTED QUOTATIONS

The famous opening verse of the Book of Esther: *"Now it came to pass in the days of Ahasuerus, this is Ahasuerus who reigned, from India to Ethiopia, over one hundred and twenty-seven provinces."*

—ESTHER 1:1

The turning point: *"Then the king Ahasuerus said to Esther the queen and to Mordecai the Jew, I have given Esther the* house of Haman; they have hanged him upon the gallows, because he sought to harm the Jews."

—ESTHER 8:7

The result of deliverance: "For the Jews there was light and happiness, joy and honor."

—ESTHER 8:16

Mordecai's instructions for celebrating the holiday: "And Mordecai wrote and sent letters to all the Jews who were in all the provinces of the king Ahasuerus, both near and far, to establish this among them, that they should keep the fourteenth day of the month Adar, and the fifteenth day of the same, yearly, as the days in which the Jews had relief from their enemies, and the month which was turned from sorrow to joy, and from mourning into gladness; that they should make them days of feasting and joy, and of sending gifts to one another and presents to the poor."

—ESTHER 9:20–22

IMPORTANT WORDS AND PHRASES

FAZUELOS: Fried thin dough made of flour and eggs, the Sephardic counterpart of hamantaschen.

GROGGER: Usually a mechanical noisemaker used in synagogues to blot out Haman's name when the Megillah is read aloud. Purim is the one day a year when decorum is relaxed in many synagogues.

HAMANTASCHEN: A tasty fruit-filled, three-cornered pastry usually thought to represent Haman's pocket or hat.

MEGILLAH: Literally a scroll, but in this case the Book of Esther. It has come to mean a long drawn-out telling of a simple story.

MISHLOACH MANOT (SHLACH MONOS IN YIDDISH): The gift of food sent to friends and neighbors.

PURIM SEUDAH: The festive meal eaten during the day on Purim.

PURIMSPIEL: Literally a Purim play. A satirical and often hilarious play performed by members of the community.

SHUSHAN PURIM: The day immediately following Purim on which the holiday is actually celebrated in Jerusalem.

PASSOVER

A JOYOUS CELEBRATION
of FREEDOM

PASSOVER

HEBREW NAME Pesach (meaning "passed over").

ALSO KNOWN AS The Holiday of Spring and the Season of Our Liberation.

WHEN IT'S CELEBRATED Passover begins on the fourteenth day of the Hebrew month of Nisan, a full moon in March or April.

WHAT IT'S ALL ABOUT Passover is a major festival (seven days in Israel and eight days among Orthodox and Conservative Jews in the Diaspora) that commemorates the liberation of the Jews from slavery in Egypt and celebrates their birth as a nation. During the holiday, Jews refrain from eating bread and other leavened products (*chametz*). On the evening of the first day (and also the second day in the

Diaspora), Jews gather with their families at home to participate in a ritual meal known as the seder and read from a traditional text called the Haggadah.

SCRIPTURAL SOURCE The Book of Exodus in the Torah recounts the story of liberation from Egypt. Rules governing the celebration are also delineated in Leviticus, Numbers, and Deuteronomy. The books of Joshua and II Kings recount celebrations of Passover led by Joshua and King Josiah, respectively. In several places in the Bible, the Jewish people are commanded to celebrate Passover for all time. For example, on the night of the Exodus, Moses commands: "You shall observe this as an ordinance for you and for your descendants forever" (EXODUS 12:24).

THE STORY After the Jews had lived in Egypt for some time (starting with Jacob and his twelve sons), a new Pharaoh assumed the throne and felt threatened by the increasingly numerous Jews. In order to prevent the Jews from gaining more power, Pharaoh first enslaved them and then tried to exterminate them by having all male children murdered at

JEWS AND THE EXODUS For the last 2,500 years or so, those celebrating Passover have referred to themselves as Jews, though the Torah never uses this term. The word *Jew* is derived from both the region Judea and from the Tribe of Judah. The term did not come into use until at least after the death of King Solomon around the tenth century B.C.E., about five hundred years after the time of the Exodus. The Exodus story in the Bible refers to the liberated people as Israelites (after Israel, the other name of the Patriarch Jacob) or Hebrews.

birth. One male baby was saved when his mother and sister placed him in a basket and floated him in the Nile River, where Pharaoh's daughter found him. She named the baby Moses (Moshe in Hebrew, which means "I drew him out of the water") and raised him in the palace as her child.

As Moses grew up, he witnessed a Jew being subjected to cruelty by an Egyptian and intervened on the Jew's behalf, killing the Egyptian. When Moses' deed was discovered, he fled into the wilderness to avoid punishment.

In the wilderness, God spoke to Moses through a bush that burned but was not consumed and instructed Moses to lead the Jews to freedom. Moses and his older brother, Aaron, went to Pharaoh to demand that he release the Jews but Pharaoh's "heart was hardened," and he made life more difficult for the Jewish slaves by increasing their workload. In order to intimidate Pharaoh into releasing the Jews, God brought Ten Plagues on Egypt:

BLOOD: The waters of the Nile River and all other streams were turned into blood.

FROGS: Egypt was overrun with frogs.

LICE: Both humans and animals suffered from lice infestation.

WILD ANIMALS: Egypt was invaded by fierce wild beasts.

DEATH OF CATTLE: Egyptian livestock became ill and died.

BOILS: Humans and animals suffered painful skin eruptions.

HAIL: Hail fell throughout the land and destroyed the Egyptian crops.

LOCUSTS: Egypt suffered an extraordinary locust invasion that destroyed everything in its path.

DARKNESS: This was not just an absence of light but a palpable darkness during day and night.

DEATH OF THE FIRSTBORN: The eldest child of every Egyptian from "the firstborn of Pharaoh who sits on his throne to the first-born of the maid-servant behind the millstone," as well as the firstborn of every Egyptian animal, all died in one night (EXODUS 11:5).

Just before the last and most terrible plague, Moses instructed the Jews to mark their doorposts with the blood of a slaughtered lamb so that the Spirit of God would "pass over" the Jewish homes and spare the Jewish children. After this plague and the loss of his own son, Pharaoh relented and directed the Jews to depart from Egypt. Concerned that Pharaoh might change his mind, the Jews left Egypt in such haste that the dough they had made for bread did not have time to rise. For that reason, Jews eat unleavened bread, matzah (or matzot), during the Festival of Passover. Shortly after the Jews quit Egypt, Pharaoh regretted his decision and chased after them with his army. The Jews were camped by the Red Sea (or possibly, a Sea of Reeds) and found themselves between the Egyptian enemy and the water. To save the Jews,

RED SEA? Does the Bible really mean that the Jews crossed the Red Sea, which separates the Sinai Peninsula in Africa from Saudi Arabia in Asia? The Bible refers to the body of water crossed by the Jews as Yam Suph, which translates as Sea of Reeds. Most scholars today think that Yam Suph refers either to the Gulf of Eilat or to a now-dried-out lake in the Sinai Peninsula. The confusion probably arose in the English translation because of the similarity of the words *red* and *reed*.

God parted the sea so they could safely cross, and then closed the waters on the pursuing Egyptians, who drowned.

THE SEDER

On the first night of Passover (and also on the second in the Diaspora), Jews gather at home with their families for the Passover meal called the seder, which literally means the "order." The seder is a celebration of liberation and freedom and is the most widely accepted ritual practice among Jews throughout the world, even among those who are not otherwise religiously observant. Through eating special foods, singing festive songs, and performing rituals to commemorate the liberation, the seder is an important way parents pass on their faith and customs to the next generation of children. In honoring this holiday and performing the mandated rituals, Jews provide the glue to bind future Jewish children to their heritage and to celebrate triumph in the face of challenges. In the Bible, Moses instructs his people: "And when your son will ask you at some future time, 'What is this?' you shall tell him, 'With a strong hand, the Lord brought us out from Egypt, from the house of bondage'" (EXODUS 13:14). The seder serves as the vehicle for transmitting this message.

THE SEDER SERVICE (BEFORE THE FESTIVE MEAL)

The seder is an elaborate meal replete with even more elaborate rituals. It is usually led by one of the adults present who calls upon others to participate in readings and song. The seder has fifteen formal sections that are followed in a prescribed sequence, beginning with a blessing over the wine and a formal invitation to anyone who needs a place at a Passover meal to join. As part of the service, a variety of foods are blessed and eaten to symbolize the road to freedom; bitter herbs are consumed to recall the bitterness of life under slavery, and matzah is eaten to bring to mind the haste with which the Israelites left Egypt, as the former slaves did not have time to let their dough rise.

THE FIFTEEN SECTIONS OF THE SEDER The rabbis designated fifteen sections of the seder, noting that the holiday falls on the fifteenth day of the Hebrew month of Nisan. The fifteen steps slow the pace in order to demonstrate that the road to freedom was slow and also in order to arouse the curiosity of children.

1. KADEISH: Traditional blessing over wine is called the Kiddush.

2. URCHATZ: The leader of the seder washes his hands.

3. KARPAS: The leader distributes a vegetable (often parsley) dipped in salt water. The salt water symbolizes the tears shed by Jews in slavery.

4. YACHATZ: The leader breaks one of the three matzot (plural of matzah) in half and sets aside one part for the *afikomen*, a piece of matzah that is the last food eaten.

5. MAGID: The leader and participants then recount the Exodus story; this section of the seder begins with a formal invitation to guests and needy persons and is followed by the Four Questions (see page 104).

6. RACHTZAH: All the participants wash their hands.

7. MOTZI: Two blessings are recited over the matzah.

8. MATZAH: The matzah is eaten.

9. MAROR: The participants eat a bitter herb or vegetable (*maror*) in commemoration of the bitterness of slavery.

10. KORECH: The leader distributes sandwiches of matzah and bitter herbs in order to remember the ancient Paschal sacrifice that was eaten in this manner in the Temple.

11. SHULCHAN ORECH: The festive meal is finally eaten.

12. TZAFUN: After the meal, the afikomen, the piece of broken matzah, is eaten as the last food of the evening.

13. BARECH: Participants recite Grace after Meals.

14. HALLEL: The participants sing songs of praise to God.

15. NIRTZAH: The seder is concluded with a prayer that the evening's service be accepted, along with an expression of hope for the Messiah.

THE HAGGADAH The script for the seder is prescribed by an ancient text called the Haggadah. There are hundreds of editions of the text, many of them beautifully illustrated with modern or ancient commentaries. At the seder, the participants read from the Haggadah, recount the story of the Exodus, and each person present is instructed to see him or herself as having personally been liberated from slavery.

SPECIAL FOODS AT THE SEDER

As with many other Jewish celebrations, special foods play a pivotal role in the seder ceremony. The participants at the seder eat matzah as a remembrance of the hasty departure from Egypt. They also eat bitter herbs to remember the bitterness of slavery, and a brown paste known as *charoset*, which is similar to Waldorf salad and usually consists of apples, nuts, and the family's secret ingredients, as a reminder of the bricks and mortar the Jews were required to make during slavery. Each participant also drinks four cups of wine (or grape juice) at prescribed times. There is a complete absence of leavened products and most grains at the seder and throughout Passover.

THE SEDER TABLE

The Passover table is elegantly set in preparation for the meal. In addition to the seder plate on the table, there are three matzot set under a cloth and a cup of wine in front of every guest, plus an extra cup of wine in the center of the table for the Prophet Elijah, who is an invited guest to the celebration. The seder plate is set in a central place on the table and has six symbolic food items.

THE SEDER PLATE The seder plate is usually a special dish or platter made of porcelain or silver that is sometimes handed down from generation to generation. The foods on the plate are:

MAROR: The bitter herb symbolizing the bitterness of slavery.

CHAROSET: A sweet brown paste representing the mortar used by the Jewish slaves in Egypt.

KARPAS: A vegetable dipped in salt water.

ZEROAH: A roasted and charred shankbone or poultry bone, symbolizing the Paschal sacrifice that was offered in the ancient Jewish Temple.

BEITZAH: A hard-boiled, charred egg representing a Temple offering that was brought with the Paschal sacrifice.

THE SEDER AND THE NUMBER FOUR

T he number four plays a prominent role in the seder. The number comes up in a variety of ways over the course of the evening.

THE FOUR QUESTIONS After the preliminary blessing of the wine and the formal invitation to guests and needy persons, the youngest child at the seder asks or sings the famous Four Questions (*Mah Nishtanah* in Hebrew). The main question is: "Why is this night different from every other night of the year?" The child then elaborates with four specific questions:

1. Why do we eat matzah and not bread?

2. Why do we eat bitter herbs?

3. Why do we dip our food in salt water or in the charoset?

4. Why do we sit like nobles and lean while we dine rather than sit upright?

Interestingly, no one ever answers the questions directly, although the entire seder ritual (and the conversations that ensue) are meant to answer them.

THE FOUR SONS Shortly after the Four Questions, the Haggadah presents an allegory of four sons who are, respectively, wise, wicked, simple, and one who cannot even ask questions. Each son asks a particular question, and in each of the four cases, the parent is required to elaborate on the Exodus and the Passover celebration with a biblical verse that speaks to the child's level. The four sons represent a cross section of Jewish youth, and the answers to the sons illustrate the parent's obligations to transmit tradition in a manner fitting the specific qualities and character of the child.

1. The wise son inquires about the specific rules of the seder by asking, "What are all the statutes, testimonies, and laws that the Lord, our God, commanded you?" The parent is to answer with some of the detailed laws of Passover.

2. The wicked son also asks about the rules but does so in a cynical, mocking tone: "What does this service mean to *you*?" The parent is advised to rebuke the wicked son and say that "the seder is performed because of what the Lord did for me when I went out of Egypt, and had you,

the wicked son, been present at the Exodus, you would not have been redeemed."

3. The simple son asks only, "What's this?" and the parent is to tell him, "With a mighty hand, the Lord brought us out of Egypt."

4. And to the one who is not even capable of asking, the parent should say the seder rituals "are on account of what God did when I came out of Egypt."

THE FOUR CUPS Over the course of the evening, each seder participant is required to drink four cups of wine (but grape juice will do). These are manifestations of joy, freedom, and prosperity, but also symbolize God's hand in the four aspects of the Exodus: removal from Egypt, rescue, redemption, and resettlement in the Promised Land.

RITUALS AND CUSTOMS

In addition to participating in the seder and reciting the Haggadah, there are several Passover rituals and customs.

THE PROHIBITION OF CHAMETZ

Chametz comprises leavened products made from wheat, rye, oats, spelt, and barley. Jews are prohibited not only from eating chametz but also from possessing it on Passover.

Many households clean their homes thoroughly before Passover to remove all leavened products that might be in their possession. They use entirely different dishes and utensils during Passover so as not to inadvertently consume chametz. The weeks before Passover are generally busy ones as people purchase special foods and clean every crevice of their home to rid it of chametz.

In order not to bear the economic loss associated with discarding dishes and food, the rabbis developed the concept of selling chametz. A household sells its chametz to a non-Jew without the specific right to purchase it back but with the definite expectation that the non-Jew will sell it back after the holiday. This way, the chametz is technically not in the Jew's possession over the holiday. In practice today, the household authorizes a local rabbi to sell the chametz to a non-Jew. The rabbi does it for the whole

THE LITTLE BOOK OF JEWISH CELEBRATIONS

community, typically to a non-Jewish clergyman or to an employee of the congregation.

Jews of Eastern European background also do not consume *kitniyot* during Passover; these are grains and legumes such as rice, corn, soybeans, string beans, peas, and lentils. However, Sephardic Jews, those who trace their ancestry to the Iberian Peninsula, do not adhere to the prohibition against kitniyot, which arose in medieval Europe, probably because of the similarity in appearance between kitniyot and the clearly prohibited grains.

ELIJAH'S CUP

Elijah the Prophet is seen in Jewish tradition as the forerunner of salvation and redemption. At the beginning of the Seder, participants pour a cup of wine and leave it on the table as an invitation to Elijah. In recent years, a tradition has also arisen to pour a cup of water in honor of the Prophetess Miriam (Moses's sister) for her role in the Exodus and the splitting of the sea.

STEALING THE AFIKOMEN

Technically, the seder cannot end until the afikomen is eaten, so a practice has arisen in which the leader of the seder allows the youngest participant to "steal" and hide the afikomen and return it for the promise of a gift. In some traditions, the leader hides the afikomen and promises a gift to the child who finds it.

SONG OF SONGS

On the Sabbath that falls within Passover, the synagogue service includes a reading of the entire Song of Songs, a beautifully written biblical book whose opening line ascribes authorship to King Solomon. The book appears to be an extended love poem but is traditionally seen as a parable of God's love for the Jewish people and is read during Passover, the time of celebrating deliverance.

SELECTED QUOTATIONS

On God's instruction to Pharaoh: *"Then the Lord said unto Moses: Go to Pharaoh and tell him: 'The Lord, the God of the Hebrews has said: Let my people go, that they may serve me.'"*
—EXODUS 9:1

On the commandment to eat matzah: *"You shall not eat leavened bread; for seven days you shall eat matzot, the bread of affliction, for you left the land of Egypt in haste."*
—DEUTERONOMY 16:3

The most famous line of the Passover Haggadah: *"Why is this night different from all other nights?"*

On God's deliverance: *"The Lord took us out of Egypt with a mighty hand and an outstretched arm, with terrible power and with signs and omens."*
—DEUTERONOMY 26:8

IMPORTANT WORDS AND PHRASES

AFIKOMEN: The final food partaken at the seder is a piece of matzah broken off at the beginning of the seder. It is thought to derive from a Greek word meaning "dessert."

CHAMETZ: Bread or other products containing grain that has been allowed to rise or ferment; all chametz is prohibited for the duration of the festival.

HAGGADAH: The book comprising the script for the seder.

MAH NISHTANAH: The first words of the Four Questions, meaning: "Why is this [night] different?"

MATZAH: The unleavened bread symbolizing the haste in which the Exodus unfolded and also the bread of affliction or poverty, in contrast to the "rich" bread consumed on Shabbat and other holidays.

PESACH: The Hebrew word for Passover, which means "passed over": God skipped over the homes of the Jews when he slew the first-born of Egypt. Pesach (or Passover) is also the name of the Paschal sacrifice brought in ancient times to the Temple in Jerusalem.

SEDER: Literally, the "order" of the festive Passover meal.

SHAVUOT

A COMMEMORATION *of the* GIVING *of the* TORAH

HEBREW NAME Shavuot in modern and Sephardic Hebrew; Shovuos or Shavuos in Ashkenazi pronunciation. The Hebrew word means "weeks."

ALSO KNOWN AS The Festival of Reaping, the Day of First Fruits, the Harvest Festival, the Time of the Giving of Our Torah, and the Festival of Weeks.

WHEN IT'S CELEBRATED Shavuot is celebrated on the sixth day of the Hebrew month of Sivan, which occurs in late May or early June. In the Diaspora, among Orthodox and Conservative Jews, Shavuot is also celebrated on the following day. Shavuot is the fiftieth day after Passover and is the culmination of the Omer period (see page 117).

WHAT IT'S ALL ABOUT Shavuot is the anniversary of the day that God gave the Ten Commandments to the nation of Israel assembled at Mount Sinai. On Passover, the Jews were liberated from slavery, and on Shavuot, they became a nation under God's dominion. On Shavuot, Jews celebrate by staying up all night and studying Torah, by reading the Book of Ruth in synagogue, and by enjoying meals that usually consist of dairy foods.

SCRIPTURAL SOURCE The narrative of the giving of the Ten Commandments is in Exodus, chapters 19 and 20. The Jews arrived in the wilderness of Sinai on the first day of the third month following the Exodus and received the commandments after several days of preparation. Leviticus chapter 23 commands the people to count fifty days from Passover and then celebrate the Festival of the First Fruits. A repetition of this commandment is found in Deuteronomy chapter 16.

THE STORY According to the account in the Book of Exodus, the weeks following liberation from Egypt were eventful, replete with new miracles and dangers. God saved His people by splitting the sea and providing safe passage as the Egyptians chased them.

He provided sustenance to the starving Jews by delivering manna from heaven, and Moses provided water to the thirsty Israelites by striking a rock. Finally, just before entering the Sinai wilderness, the weary and weak Jews fought and defeated the mighty but evil nation of Amalek. These weeks culminated with the giving of the Ten Commandments on Mount Sinai, a momentous event witnessed by the whole community and accompanied with ferocious thunder and lightning. In subsequent generations, the Festival of Weeks was celebrated by sacrifices and the offering of first fruits.

RITUALS AND CUSTOMS

Shavuot is a one- or two-day festival, unlike Passover and Sukkot, which are seven or eight days. The holiday features a synagogue service, which includes reading from the Book of Ruth, as well as dairy meals, and an all-night learning event.

COUNTING THE OMER

Other than the Temple service, which primarily involved offerings, the only biblically mandated ritual connected to Shavuot is the counting of the Omer. After the Exodus, the Jews were commanded to count seven complete weeks until the giving of the Torah. This ritual continues today as a special blessing recited each evening, beginning on the second night of Passover and ending on the day before Shavuot. The count is seen as spiritual preparation for receipt of the Torah. In postbiblical times, the forty-nine-day period of the Omer is also seen as a time of semi-mourning because many catastrophes befell the Jewish people during this period.

TIKKUN LEIL SHAVUOT

On the holiday eve, in anticipation of celebrating the giving of the Ten Commandments, members of the community engage in all-night Torah study (known as Tikkun Leil Shavuot) that concludes at dawn with the recitation of the morning service.

THE BOOK OF RUTH

The biblical Book of Ruth is read in the synagogue during the festival. Shavuot is also called the Harvest Festival, as the principal events of the Book of Ruth took place at harvest time. Ruth, a Moabite woman married to an Israelite, had returned to Moab with her husband and his family during a time of famine in Israel. When her husband died, Ruth's mother-in-law, Naomi, advised Ruth to go to her own family, but Ruth was determined to stay with Naomi and become part of the Jewish people. Ruth then married a relative of Naomi's, and the Book of Ruth ends with a recitation of Ruth's genealogy and descendants, culminating with her great-grandson, the future King David. Jewish tradition analogizes Ruth's devotion and loving-kindness to God's love of His people.

EATING DAIRY FOOD

It is customary to eat dairy foods on the holiday. There are many fanciful reasons given for this custom, though its exact origin remains unknown. One reason given is that until the Revelation at Sinai, the Jews did not have the laws pertaining to keeping a kosher diet (kashrut), including the laws of ritual slaughter. Once these laws were received, the Jews could no longer use their existing pots and dishes for meat, so they opted for dairy foods, which had fewer restrictions. In modern times, Jews eat cheesecake or blintzes or the like.

(**GREENERY AND FLOWERS**)

The synagogue and home are customarily decorated with greenery and flowers in order to honor the festival.

SELECTED QUOTATIONS

On the giving of the Ten Commandments: *"And it came to pass on the third day, when it was morning, that there was thunder and lightning and a thick cloud upon the mountain and the sound of the shofar exceedingly loud."*
—EXODUS 19:16

On the Seven Weeks: *"And you shall count for yourself from the first day after the day of rest (Passover), from that day that you brought the Omer [a sheaf offering] seven complete weeks."*
—LEVITICUS 23:15

On Ruth's devotion to her mother-in-law: *"And Ruth said, 'Do not beg me to leave you, or to refrain from following you. For where you go, I will go; and where you stay, I will stay; your people shall be my people, and your God my God: Where you die, I will die, and there will I be buried.'"*
—THE BOOK OF RUTH 1:16–17

IMPORTANT WORDS AND PHRASES

ASERET HADIBROT: Hebrew for the Ten Commandments, which were given to the Jewish people on Shavuot.

OMER: The period between Passover and Shavuot, and the count that is kept every day during that time.

TIKKUN LEIL SHAVUOT: The custom of staying up all night on the holiday and studying Torah.

THE SABBATH

THE JEWISH DAY of REST

THE SABBATH

HEBREW NAME Shabbat, or Shabbos in Yiddish and in Ashkenazi pronunciation.

ALSO KNOWN AS The Day of Rest and the Seventh Day.

WHEN IT'S CELEBRATED The Jewish Sabbath is Saturday, the seventh day of the week. It begins eighteen minutes before sunset on Friday and ends at nightfall on Saturday when three stars are (or should be) visible in the night sky.

WHAT IT'S ALL ABOUT The Sabbath is the Jewish day of rest and is one of the fundamental practices of Jewish life. Prescribed as one of the Ten Commandments, Sabbath is a remembrance of both the creation of the universe and the Exodus from Egypt. Jews refrain from work on the Sabbath, enjoy meals with their families, and recite special blessings over wine and challah, the traditional Sabbath bread. Women light candles in the home to welcome the Sabbath.

SCRIPTURAL SOURCE The commandment to keep the Sabbath is set forth many times in the Torah. God declares the Sabbath holy right in the beginning of the Torah: "God blessed the seventh day and made it holy because on it He rested from all the work which He had done in creation" (GENESIS 2:3). Sabbath observance is also incorporated in the Ten Commandments (EXODUS 20:8–11).

SABBATH OBSERVANCE IN THE TEN COMMANDMENTS Sabbath observance is mandated by the fourth of the Ten Commandments. The Torah contains two versions of the Ten Commandments, in Exodus (20:1–14) and Deuteronomy (5:6–18), and provides two distinct reasons for Sabbath observance. The Friday night blessing over the wine refers to both reasons: a commemoration of God's creation of the world and a recollection of the Exodus from Egypt.

"Remember the Sabbath day to keep it holy. Six Days shall you labor and do all your work. And the seventh day is a Sabbath to the Lord, your God; you shall do no work . . . For in six days God created the heaven and the earth, the sea and all that is in them, and He rested on the seventh day. Therefore, God blessed the Sabbath day and sanctified it." —Exodus 20:8–11

"Observe the Sabbath to sanctify it. Six days you shall labor and do all your work and the seventh day is a Sabbath to the Lord, your God; you shall do no work . . . And you shall remember that you were a slave in the land of Egypt and God took you out of there with a strong hand and an outstretched arm; therefore did the Lord your God command you to keep the Sabbath."—Deuteronomy 5:12–16

RITUALS AND CUSTOMS

Shabbat observance is centered around the home, with festive meals and blessings, and the synagogue, where uplifting services take place.

LIGHTING THE CANDLES

Observance of Shabbat begins at home on Friday night with the lighting of Shabbat candles, usually by the female head of the family. A blessing is made over the candles, the woman covers her eyes to increase concentration, and she symbolically waves the candlelight into the room to welcome the Sabbath into the home. Many families give the Shabbat candles a prominent place on their dinner table so the candles beautifully illuminate the room.

SHABBAT DINNER

After evening prayers, the family sits at the specially appointed Shabbat table. The dinner includes the performance of several rituals, some of which are repeated the following day. The table also has a goblet of wine and two loaves of bread (usually challah), covered with a cloth.

Before eating, the family sings "Shalom Aleichem," a song welcoming the angels who presumably visit the home on Friday evening. The song originated with Jewish mystics in the sixteenth or seventeenth century in the Galilee in Israel. After that song, some families sing "Eshet Chayil" ("A Woman of Valor") from the Book of Proverbs, extolling the virtues of the ideal wife.

BLESSING THE WINE The leader of the service then makes Kiddush, a prayer of sanctification over wine that recalls God's creation of heaven and earth, His resting on the seventh day, and His blessing of the Sabbath. The Kiddush denotes the Sabbath as a commemoration of creation as well as the Exodus from Egypt. The Kiddush ends with the traditional blessing over wine.

BLESSING THE CHALLAH After Kiddush, members of the family ritually wash their hands by pouring water from a vessel on each hand twice and make the blessing over

hand-washing in preparation for the meal. The leader of the service then removes the covering over the bread, which is typically two loaves of challah, a rich, festive braided loaf. Challah is usually a fluffy, golden bread made with egg as well as water. In general, challah is eaten on Shabbat and on Jewish holidays but not during the week so it retains its special quality. The leader then makes the blessing over the bread, cuts or tears the loaf, and shares the pieces with everyone around the table.

CHOLENT In addition to challah, another food often served on Shabbat is cholent, a hearty stew usually consisting of meat, beans, barley, and potatoes. The stew begins cooking before Shabbat (to observe the prohibition against cooking

THE SIGNIFICANCE OF CHALLAH

Two loaves of challah are used for the blessing as a reminder that on the Sabbath God provided the Israelites with a double portion of manna, the miraculous food that fell from heaven during the forty-year sojourn in the wilderness following the Exodus. The first blessing at the table is the Kiddush over the wine; in order not to "embarrass" the bread, which is as important as the wine, it is kept covered until it is blessed as well.

on the Sabbath) and simmers for twelve hours or more in a warm oven or stovetop so it may be eaten warm at the Shabbat day meal.

BLESSING THE CHILDREN The father and mother will then bless their children. (In some families, this blessing occurs earlier in the evening.) Boys receive the blessing Jacob gave to his grandchildren, which he predicted future generations would use to bless their own children: "May God

make you like Ephraim and Manasseh [the sons of Joseph]."
Girls are blessed: "May God make you like Sarah, Rebecca,
Rachel, and Leah [the Matriarchs]."

SABBATH SERVICES

Although Jews are required to pray three times each day, Friday night and Sabbath morning services are the most widely attended. The Friday night service, called Kabbalat Shabbat (Reception of the Sabbath), is filled with psalms and joyous songs, including the rousing "Lecha Dodi" (Come, My Friend), which equates the Sabbath with a beautiful bride.

Celebrations, such as bar and bat mitzvahs and the calling of the groom to the Torah before his wedding, are generally centered around Saturday morning services. The Shabbat service consists of a morning service (Shacharit), the reading of the weekly Torah portion (called the parashah) and the haftorah, and an additional service (Musaf) reminiscent of the extra service in the ancient Temple.

After morning services in the synagogue, the family gathers for the second Shabbat meal, which is preceded by a Kiddush that is shorter than Friday night's, and the blessing over the challahs.

ENDING SHABBAT

In the evening, when it is so dark that at least three stars are visible (or would be in case of cloud cover), a family member leads the brief Havdalah (literally, "separation") service, which declares the end of the Sabbath. Blessings are made over wine, over a flame to mark God's creation of light, and over sweet-smelling spices as a wish for a sweet week ahead. As in many other Jewish ceremonies, Elijah the Prophet is symbolically invited to the service and many families sing a hymn to Elijah.

ABSTAINING FROM WORK

Many of those who observe the Shabbat find it a welcome respite from intense weekday activities because of the prohibition against performing "work." Jewish law (halachah) pertaining to Sabbath observance defines work not only as active labor providing compensation, but as other forms of deliberate activity. The Talmud identifies thirty-nine main categories of prohibited work, which include cooking, writing, sewing, and many other tasks that do not require particular exertion but that involve an act of creation. One of the prohibited activities is lighting a fire. Orthodox and some Conservative Jews include within that prohibition the active use of electric devices, so while they can enjoy the lighting provided by electricity, they will not switch lights on or off. Similarly, they will not ride in automobiles or other forms of transportation, and they will not use the telephone or watch television. Many Jews do not have such a strict interpretation of Sabbath prohibitions, and there is a great range of observance even among traditional Jews.

Even those who strictly observe the prohibition against work on the Sabbath provide an exception for reasons of health or to aid others who need assistance for reasons of health. This covers any serious illness, health condition, or injury, as well as in case of fire or other emergencies, and is not limited to life-threatening situations.

THE THIRTY-NINE FORMS OF "WORK" The Talmud identifies thirty-nine specific forms of work that are prohibited on the Sabbath. These are based on the types of labor that were employed in building the Tabernacle after the Exodus. The list includes kindling a fire, planting, reaping, writing, and baking. In modern times, many subcategories have been included as a result of new inventions, such as closing an electric circuit to initiate electric power and typing on a computer.

SELECTED QUOTATIONS

On the conclusion of creation: *"God blessed the seventh day and made it holy because on it He rested from all the work which He had done in creation."*
—GENESIS 2:1–3

From "Lecha Dodi," sung during the Friday evening service: *"Come my beloved to greet the bride, to greet the Sabbath's presence."*

From the Friday evening service and the Saturday morning Kiddush: *"And the children of Israel shall keep the Sabbath, to perform the Sabbath, for all their generations, an eternal covenant between the children of Israel and me. It is a sign forever, for in six days God created the heaven and the earth and on the seventh day, He rested and was refreshed."*

IMPORTANT WORDS AND PHRASES

CHALLAH: Special bread eaten on Shabbat and holidays.

HAVDALAH: The brief service after nightfall on Saturday marking the end of Shabbat.

KABBALAT SHABBAT: The Friday evening service.

KIDDUSH: The blessing over wine made on the Sabbath.

"LECHA DODI": Hebrew song recited at Friday night services, literally meaning "Come, My Friend."

PARASHAH: The weekly portion of the Torah reading.

SHABBAT SHALOM: Hebrew greeting on Shabbat, meaning "peaceful Shabbat."

RITES OF PASSAGE

In addition to Jewish holidays, major lifecycle events are marked by religious services coupled with joyous festivities that call upon the community to unite and celebrate. A baby boy is welcomed into the faith eight days after birth by circumcision at a ceremony called the Brit Milah (Covenant of Circumcision). A baby girl is honored shortly after birth by a Simchat Bat (Celebration of the Daughter). At both of these occasions, the Jewish community comes together to recite prayers, hear the child's Hebrew name, and partake in a festive celebration.

Adolescent boys and girls are welcomed into the religious community at bar mitzvah and bat mitzvah ceremonies. The young man or woman typically undertakes an important synagogue role, such as reading from the Torah or teaching on a religious subject. After this momentous occasion, the young person is deemed to have accepted all the religious responsibilities and obligations of an adult and may be counted in the quorum necessary for communal prayer.

A Jewish wedding is both a religious and a legal ceremony that binds together a bride and groom to start their Jewish life together. The event takes place under a wedding canopy (chuppah) and is replete with blessings and ritual. At the same time, the groom undertakes the specific legal obligation of supporting and sustaining his bride under the terms of an ancient formulation of a marriage contract (*ketubah*). After the ceremony, guests honor the bride and groom with joyous singing and dancing and, of course, a festive meal. Read on for more on these once-in-a-lifetime special events.

CIRCUMCISION

BRINGING *the* MALE CHILD *into the* COVENANT *of* ABRAHAM

CIRCUMCISION

HEBREW NAME Brit Milah (Covenant of Circumcision).

ALSO KNOWN AS The circumcision ritual is often referred to simply as Brit, and in Yiddish and in Ashkenazi pronunciation, it is called bris.

WHEN IT'S CELEBRATED The Brit takes place on the baby boy's eighth day of life. It may take place even on the Sabbath or on a holiday, including Yom Kippur, the holiest holiday. Note that a Jewish day begins and ends at sunset. If the baby is born on Sunday night after dark, he is considered to have been born on Monday, and the Brit will take place on the following Monday, rather than on Sunday. Also, the Brit is always postponed for reasons of the baby's health including premature birth and any medical complication; if the Brit is postponed, it is performed as soon as the baby's doctor and the mohel deem it safe.

WHAT IT'S ALL ABOUT The Brit Milah is performed by a ritual circumciser called a mohel. The ceremony is usually performed in the presence of family and guests and is followed by a celebratory meal called a Seudat Mitzvah (Meal of the Commandment). The Brit is always performed in daylight hours and can be held in any suitable location but is usually held in a synagogue or in a family home.

SCRIPTURAL SOURCE In Genesis, God commanded Abraham and his descendants to be circumcised: "This is My covenant, which you shall keep, between Me and your descendants: every male among you shall be circumcised. And you shall be circumcised in the flesh of your foreskin; and it shall be a token of the covenant between Me and you" (GENESIS 17:10–13).

THE COVENANT The scriptural reference to circumcision in Genesis chapter 17 calls circumcision a "token of the covenant." The actual covenant was God's promise to Abraham to multiply greatly, to be a father of a multitude of nations, to be a God to him and his descendants throughout their generations, and finally, to give to him and his descendants the land of Canaan for an everlasting possession. The circumcision ceremony is the human response to these promises and constitutes the "seal of the covenant."

RITUALS AND CUSTOMS

THE CEREMONY

The circumcision ceremony is the fulfillment of the father's biblically mandated obligation to circumcise his eight-day-old son. The father delegates that responsibility to the mohel. During the ceremony, the baby is

passed from his parents to the mohel by a specially designated relative or guest, and another designated relative or
guest holds the baby during the circumcision. At the end
of the ceremony, the baby's name is announced.

BLESSINGS AND PRAYERS AT THE BRIT MILAH The ceremony begins with a declaration of welcome both to the
newborn and to Elijah the Prophet, who is considered an
invisible guest at the circumcision.

A person honored as the *kvater* brings the baby from
the mother to the father, who in turns gives the baby
to the mohel.

The mohel places the baby on the thighs or knees of
the person honored as the *sandek*, who holds the baby during the circumcision.

Before the circumcision, the mohel makes the
blessing: "Blessed art Thou Lord, our God, King of the universe, who has sanctified us with His commandments and
commanded us concerning circumcision."

Immediately after the circumcision, the father of the
infant recites the blessing: "Blessed art Thou Lord, our
God, King of the universe, who has sanctified us with His

commandments and commanded us to enter my son into the Covenant of Abraham, our Father."

NAMING THE BABY After these blessings, the mohel or another guest makes the traditional blessing over wine. The father and mother tell the person making the blessing the Hebrew name they are giving the child. The name is announced and the guests go on to participate in the festive meal. In many communities, the child is often named for a departed loved one. In Sephardic communities, however, children are often named for living relatives.

THE FESTIVE MEAL After the ceremony the guests are encouraged to participate in a festive meal (Seudat Mitzvah), which is actually part of the Brit itself, and afterward, a special Grace after Meals is recited.

SELECTED QUOTATIONS

Biblical reference to circumcision: *"And on the eighth day the flesh of his foreskin shall be circumcised."*
—LEVITICUS 12:3

The response of guests and relatives to the blessing after the circumcision: *"Just as he has entered the covenant, so may he be introduced to the Torah, to the marriage canopy, and to a life of good deeds."*

IMPORTANT WORDS AND PHRASES

BRIT MILAH: Hebrew for "Covenant of Circumcision."

KVATER: The person who brings the baby from the mother to the father, who, in turn, gives the baby to the mohel.

MOHEL: A person specially trained in the practice of circumcision.

SANDEK: A person who holds the baby on this thighs or knees during the circumcision ceremony.

SEUDAT MITZVAH: The festive meal immediately following the circumcision and is considered part of the ceremony.

SIMCHAT BAT

BRINGING the NEWBORN GIRL into the JEWISH COMMUNITY

SIMCHAT BAT

HEBREW NAME Simchat Bat (Celebration of the Daughter).

ALSO KNOWN AS Zeved Habat, "Gift of the Daughter" (particularly in the Sephardic tradition), and Brit Habat, "Covenant of the Daughter."

WHEN IT'S CELEBRATED There is no specific time for the celebration of the Simchat Bat, but it is usually performed within the first month or two of the baby girl's birth.

WHAT IT'S ALL ABOUT In Ashkenazi communities, the Simchat Bat is a relatively new ceremony originating in the second half of the twentieth century. Sephardic communities have long celebrated the Zeved Habat. In both cases, the ceremony is seen as the parallel of the Brit Milah, the circumcision ceremony for boys, and the occasion for formally announcing the Hebrew name of the baby girl.

SCRIPTURAL SOURCE Since it is a relatively recent custom, there is no scriptural source for the Simchat Bat.

RITUALS AND CUSTOMS

There is no set procedure for the Simchat Bat, so parents have a great deal of flexibility in creating their own meaningful ceremony. Most celebrations include the blessing over wine, the formal naming of the baby girl, the recitation of relevant biblical verses, and a celebratory meal.

It is also the custom for the father of the newborn girl to be called to the Torah on the Shabbat after the birth to announce the baby's name in the synagogue. At that time, the father also makes a prayer for the health and well-being of the baby and the mother.

SELECTED QUOTATIONS

From the Sephardic Zeved Habat service: *"He who blessed our matriarchs Sarah, Rebecca, Rachel and Leah, and Miriam, and Queen Esther, may He bless this dear girl, and let her name be called* [the name of the girl], *the daughter of* [the names of the mother and father], *in good fortune and prosperity, and may she be brought up in health, peace, and tranquility. May her parents merit to share in her times of rejoicing and in her marriage, in sons and daughters, with wealth and honor."*

Traditional blessing for girls (also said every Shabbat): *"May God make you as Sarah, Rebecca, Rachel, and Leah."*

IMPORTANT WORDS
AND PHRASES

SIMCHAT BAT: Hebrew for "Celebration of the Daughter," the ceremony welcoming the newborn girl into the Jewish Community.

ZEVED HABAT: The Sephardic name for the ceremony meaning "Gift of the Daughter." The word "zeved" is derived from the matriarch Leah's blessing of thanksgiving after the birth of a child.

MISHEBERACH: The prayer for health and well-being of the mother and daughter recited at the ceremony.

BAR & BAT MITZVAH

A COMING-*of*-AGE CEREMONY

BAR & BAT MITZVAH

HEBREW NAME Bar mitzvah for boys, bat mitzvah for girls (meaning the "son" or "daughter of the commandment").

WHEN IT'S CELEBRATED A young man's bar mitzvah is celebrated when he is thirteen years old. In the Orthodox tradition, a girl's bat mitzvah is celebrated when she is twelve years old. In other streams of Jewish observance (Conservative, Reform, Reconstructionist), a girl's bat mitzvah is celebrated at age thirteen.

WHAT IT'S ALL ABOUT The bar or bat mitzvah is an exciting time for a young person, since, upon reaching the required age, the young person has technically become an adult and is accountable for his or her own Jewish obligations. A bar or bat mitzvah has two meanings: First, it refers to the young person himself or herself, having attained the requisite age. Second, it is the ceremony and celebration surrounding the milestone. At that age, the young person is required to fast on Yom Kippur and is eligible to participate in all aspects of Jewish life, including being counted as an adult in a minyan (the quorum of ten required for communal prayer). On becoming a bar or bat mitzvah, the young person usually participates in a synagogue service, reading from the Torah and/or giving a speech that includes a Torah lesson (known in Hebrew as a *D'Var Torah*). Customarily, this is followed immediately or some days later by a joyous celebration with family and friends.

SCRIPTURAL SOURCE There is no scriptural source for bar and bat mitzvah. In fact, the Torah stipulates the age of adulthood for males as twenty for purposes of the census and military service (NUMBERS 1:3). However, there are several Talmudic references to thirteen as being the age of religious responsibility, and these constitute the source for setting the time for the celebration.

RITUALS AND CUSTOMS

Bar and bat mitzvah ceremonies and celebrations mark an important rite of passage and involve several undertakings.

READING THE TORAH AND HAFTORAH

A young man or woman (except in Orthodox synagogues where girls do not participate in the service to the same extent) prepares for the bar or bat mitzvah by studying all or part of the weekly portion to be read in the synagogue on the day of the celebration. The boy or girl reads from the Torah scroll, which is written in Hebrew block letters without vowels. The reading is in the form of a chant with a special tune used only for the weekly Torah portion. The young man or woman may also chant the haftorah, which is the weekly reading from a book of the Prophets (such as Samuel, Kings, or Isaiah).

Reading the Torah and haftorah is a significant undertaking for a young person, requiring months of preparation to remember the tunes and vowels. Reading the Torah demonstrates the readiness of the bar or bat mitzvah to assume responsibility within the community.

In the Orthodox tradition, men and women do not sit together, and women and girls do not lead the prayer service or read from the Torah. In the last two generations, however, some Orthodox girls have learned to read the Torah and may read their weekly portion at an all-women's service.

TORAH LESSON

In addition to reading from the Torah, the bar mitzvah boy or bat mitzvah girl may also deliver a D'Var Torah (literally, "word" of Torah), which is a short sermon on a topic contained in the weekly reading or relating to some aspect of the Torah.

BLESSING THE BAR/BAT MITZVAH

In the synagogue or at the subsequent celebration, the parents (or the rabbi) bless the child with the ancient priestly blessing. On the day of the bar or bat mitzvah, the parents, in synagogue, also make an unusual blessing thanking God for relieving them of the burden of the child's religious obligations, since henceforth the child has his or her own responsibilities.

───────────(**BAR/BAT MITZVAH PARTIES**)───────────┤

M ore often than not, the bar or bat mitzvah celebration will include a festive party for the boy or girl's family and friends. These parties are sometimes lavish affairs and include singing and traditional Jewish and contemporary dancing.

GIFTS   Boys and girls celebrating their bar/bat mitzvah usually receive many gifts from friends and family. Many families use the occasion of the bar/bat mitzvah to introduce to young people the importance of giving charity, thereby observing the commandment of *tzedakah*. The young person is encouraged to give a portion of his or her gifts (or their equivalent value) to a Jewish charity or to one benefiting society as a whole.

(**WEARING TEFILLIN**)

O bservant Jewish men and some women don phylacteries (known in Hebrew as tefillin) each weekday during morning prayers. Tefillin consist of two leather straps, each attached to a box containing passages from the Torah. One strap goes on the left arm (for right-handed persons) and the other on the head. The word *tefillin* is derived from *tefillah*, the Hebrew word for "prayer." They are also known as phylacteries, from the ancient Greek word for "guard" or "protect."

Before their bar mitzvahs, Orthodox and Conservative boys will receive their own tefillin, and they are obligated to wear them each morning following the bar mitzvah.

SELECTED QUOTATIONS

On the bar mitzvah at age thirteen: *"Rabbi Judah, the son of Tema said: 'At five years, the child should begin to study Bible text; at ten years, the Mishnah, at thirteen, the fulfillment of the commandments . . .'"*
—ETHICS OF THE FATHERS 5:24 (A VOLUME OF THE MISHNAH DATING TO THE SECOND CENTURY C.E.)

The Priestly Blessing pronounced on the bar or bat mitzvah boy or girl: *"May God bless you and protect you. May God make His face shine on you and be gracious to you. May God favor you and grant you peace."*
—NUMBERS 6:24–26

The special blessing recited by parents when their child becomes a bar/bat mitzvah: *"Blessed be the Lord who relieved me of this burden."*

On the commandment to wear tefillin (phylacteries): *"You shall bind them for a sign on your arm and they shall be as frontlets between your eyes."*
—DEUTERONOMY 6:8

IMPORTANT WORDS AND PHRASES

BAR/BAT MITZVAH: Son or daughter of commandments. The terms refer to a child who has reached the prescribed age of maturity. It is also the name of the celebration of that event.

D'VAR TORAH: A short discourse on a Torah topic, often on the weekly portion.

HAFTORAH: The reading from the Prophets that follows the Torah reading in the synagogue.

MINYAN: The quorum of ten adults (males only in the Orthodox tradition) needed for communal prayer. Upon reaching bar/bat mitzvah age, the young person may be counted toward the minyan.

MITZVAH: A commandment.

TZEDAKAH: Derived from the Hebrew word meaning "righteousness," tzedakah has come to mean "charity."

JEWISH WEDDING

A RELIGIOUS *and* SOCIAL
MARRIAGE CEREMONY

JEWISH WEDDING

HEBREW NAME Chatunah (derived from *chatan*, the Hebrew word for "bridegroom").

WHEN IT'S CELEBRATED Jewish weddings may be performed on most weekdays, but they are not performed on the Sabbath, Jewish holidays, and fast days. Weddings are also not performed during most of the Omer period between Passover and Shavuot and during three weeks in the summer between two fast days. The Omer period and the three weeks are considered periods of semi-mourning.

WHAT IT'S ALL ABOUT A Jewish wedding comprises both a contractual commitment and a religious component. The ceremony takes place under a wedding canopy called a chuppah. Various blessings are recited under the chuppah, and the husband's contractual obligation is read aloud.

SCRIPTURAL SOURCE The Jewish wedding ceremony has followed the same basic course for thousands of years. The particulars of the ceremony derive from the Talmud and other rabbinic sources. The Bible itself does not define the ceremony but has many references to marriage.

The first commandment in the Bible is God's direction to Adam and Eve: "Be fruitful and multiply, fill the earth and master it" (GENESIS 1:28). Just after this commandment, the Torah declares: "Therefore shall a man leave his father and his mother and cling to his wife and become one flesh" (GENESIS 2:24).

The Bible sets an example of the ideal marriage in the union of Isaac and Rebecca: "Isaac then brought her into the tent of his mother Sarah, and he took Rebecca as his wife. Isaac loved her . . . " (GENESIS 24:67).

The Bible sanctifies marriage by prohibiting adultery within the Ten Commandments (EXODUS 20:13) and by delineating a list of prohibited incestuous unions (LEVITICUS 18).

RITUALS AND CUSTOMS

The Jewish wedding is both sacred and joyful and features rituals that have remained almost unchanged for millennia.

THE WEDDING CEREMONY The ceremony is a beautiful service replete with symbolism. The ceremony has several ritual components including the giving of a ring by the groom to the bride, the signing and reading of a contract defining the groom's obligations, the recital of several blessings, and the breaking of a glass.

THE MARRIAGE DOCUMENTS Before the ceremony, the bride and groom separately greet their guests, and the two formal marriage documents are signed by witnesses. The first (called the *tenaim*) is actually an engagement contract; in prior times, it was executed weeks or months before the wedding, though it is now commonplace to sign it at the wedding. The second and more important document is the *ketubah*, which is a two-thousand-year-old form of contract. It is written in Aramaic, the language of the Talmud and the everyday language spoken in the Holy Land during the Second Temple period. The ketubah delineates the husband's legal obligation to honor, feed, and support his wife. Many couples commission a decorative ketubah with beautiful calligraphy and design, which is later framed and displayed in their home.

COVERING THE BRIDE After the ketubah is signed, the groom is escorted by friends and family to the bride's reception area where he places a veil over the bride's face. This romantic tradition, called *bedeken*, is based on the biblical narrative of Jacob, who was tricked by his father-in-law, Laban, into marrying Leah instead of her sister,

Rachel, because he did not see his bride's face prior to marriage. After the groom assures himself that he has seen his bride (*kallah* in Hebrew), he covers her face with a veil, setting her apart from all other women. The ceremony is then ready to begin.

THE CHUPPAH The wedding ceremony takes place under the chuppah, an often ornately decorated wedding canopy that is open on all four sides, symbolizing the open and welcoming home the bride and groom intend to build together. The groom enters the canopy first, and when the bride arrives, she circles the groom seven times, symbolizing their protection of one another; at some weddings, the groom also circles the bride.

The religious component of the ceremony then follows and is broken into two parts, which today occur sequentially at the wedding. The ceremony begins with the first part, *kiddushin* (betrothal, sometimes also called *erusin*). The rabbi leading the ceremony recites two blessings: the traditional blessing over wine and a blessing acknowledging that God is a partner in sanctifying the marriage;

JEWISH WEDDING ⁅ 169 ⁆

the second blessing ends with the phrase, "Blessed are You, O Lord our God, King of the universe, who sanctifies His people, Israel, by means of the wedding canopy and consecrated marriage."

The groom then takes a ring and places it on the bride's forefinger on the right hand and recites the ancient prescription for marriage: "With this ring, you are wedded to me in accordance with the law of Moses and Israel." In many modern wedding ceremonies, the bride also places a ring on the groom's finger and recites: "With this ring I am wedded to you in accordance with the laws of Moses and Israel."

The ketubah is then read in Aramaic and often summarized in English as well. From a religious point of view, the couple is now legally married under Jewish law and the ceremony proceeds to the second part, called *nissuin* (marriage). Seven blessings celebrating the marriage are recited by the rabbi or by invited guests. The blessings focus on God's creation of humanity and the union of man and woman. At the conclusion of the blessings, the couple drinks from a single cup of wine to seal their union.

THE SEVEN BLESSINGS RECITED UNDER THE CANOPY The blessings recited under the contract are listed in the Talmud, which was completed no later than the fifth century C.E., but these blessings are almost certainly several centuries older.

1. "Blessed art Thou, O Lord our God, King of the universe, who creates the fruit of the vine."

2. "Blessed art Thou, O Lord our God, who created everything for His glory."

3. "Blessed art Thou, O Lord our God, King of the universe, creator of mankind."

4. "Blessed art Thou, O Lord our God, King of the universe, who created man in His image, as a mirror of His form, and formed from him an everlasting structure. Blessed art Thou, O Lord, creator of man." (Note: The "everlasting structure" is probably a reference to womankind, as God formed Eve from Adam's rib, and the everlasting structure probably refers to the institution of marriage as well.)

5. "The barren mother [a reference to Jerusalem] will sing joyfully as her children return to her in happiness. Blessed are You, O Lord our God, King of the universe, who gladdens Zion with her children."

6. "Grant much joy to these loving companions, just as You made Your creatures [Adam and Eve] happy in the Garden of Eden in time gone by. Blessed are You, O Lord our God, King of the universe, who makes the groom and bride happy."

7. "Blessed are You, O Lord our God, King of the universe, who created joy and happiness, groom and bride, gladness, joyful song, delight and cheer, love and brotherhood, peace, and companionship. Lord, our God, may we soon hear in the hills of Judah and the courtyards of Jerusalem the sounds of joy and happiness, the voices of the groom and bride, the joyous sounds of grooms under their wedding canopies, and young people in their song-filled celebrations. Blessed are You, O Lord our God, King of the universe, who gladdens the groom with the bride."

BREAKING THE GLASS   Before the ceremony concludes and the couple leaves the chuppah, the groom ceremoniously breaks a glass by stepping on it. This act reminds us that we must always temper our joy in our happiness and that we must also remember the destruction of the Temple in keeping with the Psalmist's command: "If I forget you, O Jerusalem, let my right hand wither, let my tongue stick to my palate if I cease to think of you, if I do not keep Jerusalem in memory even at my happiest hour" (PSALMS 137:5).

The ceremony ends and the bride and groom are escorted to a private room so that they can spend a few moments alone. A festive meal then follows with singing and dancing and a special Grace after meals, which repeats the Seven Blessings recited under the chuppah.

───(OTHER CUSTOMS)───

S EPARATION It is a custom in many Jewish communities that the bride and groom do not see each other for a week before the wedding until the bedeken.

AUFRUF: (Yiddish for "calling up") On the Sabbath before the wedding, the groom is called to the Torah and recites the traditional blessings before and after the reader chants from the weekly portion.

SHEVA BRACHOT: (Hebrew for Seven Blessings) During the week following the wedding, the bride and groom are feted at dinners and parties. At the Grace after Meals at these events, the same Seven Blessings that were recited under the canopy are reprised and the bride and groom again share a cup of wine.

"ESHET CHAYIL" ("A WOMAN OF VALOR"): At some weddings, after the ceremony and while the guests are assembled, the groom will serenade his bride by singing the hymn "Eshet Chayil" from chapter 31 of the Book of Proverbs, a romantic testament to the qualities of the ideal wife.

SELECTED QUOTATIONS

From the Seven Blessings recited under the wedding canopy: *"Blessed are You, O Lord our God, King of the universe, who created joy and happiness, groom and bride, gladness, joyful song, delight and cheer, love and brotherhood, peace and companionship."*

On placing the ring on the bride's finger, the groom recites: *"With this ring you are wedded to me in accordance with the laws of Moses and Israel."*

From the traditional text of the ketubah: *"Be my wife according to the law of Moses and Israel. I will work, honor, feed, and support you in the custom of Jewish men, who work, honor, feed, and support their wives faithfully."*

The opening line of the "Eshet Chayil" hymn often sung by the groom to his bride: *"A woman of worth, who can find? Her value is far beyond rubies."*

IMPORTANT WORDS AND PHRASES

AUFRUF: (Yiddish for "calling up") On the Sabbath before the wedding, the groom is called to the Torah and recites the traditional blessings.

BEDEKEN: Literally "covering," the ceremony in which the groom covers the bride's face with a veil before approaching the chuppah.

CHATAN: The Hebrew word for "groom."

CHATUNAH: The Hebrew word for "wedding ceremony."

CHUPPAH: The canopy under which the wedding ceremony is performed.

KALLAH: The Hebrew word for "bride."

KETUBAH: The legal document that delineates the husband's responsibility to his wife.

SHEVA BRACHOT: The Seven Blessings recited under the wedding canopy and at special meals during the week following the marriage.

(INDEX)